This is one brave and bold book that's as vulnerable as it is practical. No one knows His Word, His women, and His way quite like Lysa TerKeurst. And once I started reading? I couldn't stop.

—ANN VOSKAMP, bestselling author of *One Thousand Gifts*

Lysa approaches raw emotions in a way that will make every woman sigh with relief that she's not alone. Her teaching on making imperfect progress is insightful and realistic. Whether you are a stuffer or exploder or a combination of both, this is a book I highly recommend.

—TIM CLINTON, president of American Association of Christian Counselors and bestselling author of *Breakthrough*

Lysa's book will help thousands plot a successful course and react to reality in ways far beyond their fickle and unreliable emotions.

—STEPHEN ARTERBURN, host of NewLife Live and author of *Is This the One?*

We live in an age where we tend to be ruled by our emotions. If we feel it, we say it or do it. In order to live an abundant life we need to manage our emotions, not be ruled by them. Lysa gives us practical keys on how to make choices that lead to life, not death.

—CHRISTINE CAINE, founder of The A21 Campaign and author of *Undaunted*

This is a book that any mom, any wife, any woman will relate to. Lysa is transparent about the realities of living life as a real woman in a real world. Her honest struggles offer a lifeline to us all.

—SHEILA WALSH, author of *God Loves Broken People and Those Who Pretend They're N*

I was totally convicted about building barriers. I had no idea that was what I was doing or even the reasons I was doing it. You helped bring clarity; I believe it will help me learn to speak up honestly but lovingly, instead of stuffing my feelings inside.

—Buffi Y.

I had an "aha" moment in every paragraph. I highlighted everything that spoke to me, and my book now looks like a Christmas tree.

—Tracy C.

This book made me think about how I react to things and that I not only have a choice but a clear, precise action plan to change things with the help of God.

—Michelle C.

I have worked thirty years in an all-male related field and have experienced a lot of discrimination in my career. After reading this book, I confronted the president of the company about remarks he has made about me in front of other men. I was calm, chose my words wisely and confidently, with no unglued reaction. I handled my raw emotions with soul integrity!

—Kelly W.

I have five young children, which means someone always needs my attention and my house is never quiet. I've never been a screamer, but I realize I've always been unglued. This book helped me realize the damage stuffing can do.

—Jill B.

As a fiftysomething, with no children, I still am overwhelmed with how Lysa relates to all women and family situations, relationships, and personal reactions. I saw myself in so many pages of this book.

—Laura S.

Having to sit down and figure out exactly what triggers my reactions was not fun, but very enlightening. I feel like now I can start working on becoming a woman who is more in control, more connected to myself.

—Shannon B.

UNGLUED

MAKING WISE CHOICES
IN THE MIDST OF RAW EMOTIONS

LYSA TERKEURST

ZONDERVAN.com/
AUTHORTRACKER
follow your favorite authors

ZONDERVAN

Unglued
Copyright © 2012 by Lysa TerKeurst

This title is also available as a Zondervan ebook. Visit www.zondervan.com/ebooks.

This title is also available in a Zondervan audio edition. Visit www.zondervan.fm.

Requests for information should be addressed to:

Zondervan, *Grand Rapids, Michigan 49530*

Library of Congress Cataloging-in-Publication Data

TerKeurst, Lysa.
      Unglued : making wise choices in the midst of raw emotions / Lysa TerKeurst.
        p. cm.
      Includes bibliographical references (p.   ).
      ISBN 978-0-310-33279-4 (softcover)
      1. Christian women — Religious life. 2. Decision making — Religious aspects
   — Christianity. 3. Choice (Psychology) — Religious aspects — Christianity. 4. Emotions
   — Religious aspects — Christianity. I. Title.
      BV4527.T463   2012
      248.8´43 — dc23   2012005832

Published in association with the literary agency of Fedd & Company, Inc., Post Office Box 341973, Austin, TX 78734.

Cover design: Curt Diepenhorst
Cover photography: Helena Inkera / Getty Images®
Interior design: Beth Shagene

Printed in the United States of America

12 13 14 15 16 17 18 /DCI/ 23 22 21 20 19 18 17 16 15 14 13 12 11 10 9 8 7 6 5 4 3 2 1

*What happens in between the smiling snapshots
of life isn't all pretty.
I'm willing to admit that.
And I love my friends who are brave enough
to admit the messy stuff as well.
I dedicate these words to you as we set out
to make some imperfect progress together.*

Contents

Acknowledgments

With deep appreciation I say thank you to the precious people listed below. While only my name is listed as the author, each of these dear souls played a vital role in the development of this message. Many of them have lived with me through the ups and downs of my own messy, unglued times. And they still love me.

What sweet grace. I treasure each of you so much.

My favorites: Art, Jackson, Hope, Mark, Ashley, and Brooke — You are the answers to the prayers I prayed as a little girl.

LeAnn Rice, Renee Swope, Karen Ehman, Holly Good, Genia Rogers, Mary Ann Ruff, and Amy King — Amazing friends, beautiful leaders.

Glynnis Whitwer — Encourager and a great word untangler. Is that a word? Smiles.

The Proverbs 31 Team — Soul sisters.

Elevation Church, Pastor and Holly, Chunks, and Amy — You weave transforming truth into my life. Thank you for your constant support and terrific leadership.

Meredith Brock, Jennie Stills, and Lindsay Kreis — Gifts from God.

Nicki Koziarz, Samantha Reed, and Melissa Taylor — Precious servants and wonderful cheerleaders.

Laci Watson — In the Loop Group leader extraordinaire.

Cile Wison — Researcher and wonderful friend.

Tina Clark and Lisa Cheramie — You make the simple places where I write, beautiful.

Jenny Reynolds and Shaunti Feldhahn — Two of the smartest women I know!

Esther Fedorkevich and Sandy Vander Zicht — More than an agent and an editor, you are precious friends.

Scott Macdonald, Tracy Danz, Don Gates, Alicia Mey, and Greg Clouse — It is a dream working with all of my Zondervan friends. You aren't just a publisher; you are my true partners in ministry.

An Invitation
to Imperfect Progress

Emotions aren't bad. But try telling that to my brain at 2:08 a.m. when I should be sleeping instead of mentally beating myself up.

Why had I become completely unglued about bathroom towels? Towels, for heaven's sake. *Towels!*

The master bathroom is the favorite bathroom in our house. Although my three girls share a small bathroom upstairs, they much prefer our more spacious bathroom downstairs. As a result, our bath towels are frequently hijacked. I'll hop out of the tub and reach for the freshly laundered towel I hung on the rack the day before only to discover it isn't there. Ugh. So, I wind up using a hand towel. (A hand towel. Can you feel my pain?) And while using said hand towel, I am muttering under my breath, "I'm banning the girls from our bathroom." Then, of course, I never do anything to make the situation better. And the same scene repeats itself time and time again.

I'd been dealing with the bath towel, or lack thereof, situation for quite a while before Art got involved. Up to this point, he had somehow managed to escape the woes of using a hand towel. But not this day. And his happiness did not abound upon discovering nothing but air where the towel should have been.

Since I happened to be nearby, he asked if I might please go get him a towel. I marched upstairs, convinced I'd find every towel we own strewn randomly about in my girls' rooms. I was preparing a little scolding speech as I marched, marched, marched up the stairs. With each step I felt more and more stern. But when I went from room to room, there were no towels. None. How could this be? Completely baffled, I then went into the laundry room. Nope, no towels there either. What in the world? Meanwhile, I felt a tightening knot of tension in my neck as Art again called out for a towel.

"I'm coming, for heaven's sake," I snapped back as I walked to the linen closet where the beach towels are kept.

"You'll just have to use one of these," I said, tossing a large Barbie beach towel over the shower door.

"What?" he asked, "Isn't this the towel the dogs sleep on?"

"Oh good gracious, it was clean and folded in the linen closet. I wouldn't give you a towel the dogs had been on!" Now my voice came out high-pitched, and it was clear I was really annoyed.

"Uggghhhh. Is it too much to ask for a clean towel?" Art was asking a question, but to me it was more like a statement. A judgment. Of me.

"Why do you always do that?!" I screamed. "You take simple mistakes and turn them into slams against me! Did I take the towels and hide them who-knows-where? *No!* Did I let the dogs sleep on the Barbie towel? *No!* And furthermore, that isn't the Barbie towel the dogs were sleeping on. We have *three* Barbie towels — so there! Now you have the dadgum 4-1-1 on the towel issue. And none of this is my fault!"

I headed upstairs in a huff to give the girls a piece of my mind. "Never! Ever! Ever! You are *not* allowed to use the towels in our bathroom ever, ever, ever *again!* Do you understand me?!" The girls just looked at me, dumbfounded that I was getting this upset over towels, and then started profusely declaring that they didn't have said towels.

Back downstairs, I grabbed my purse, slammed the door, and screeched the tires as I angrily peeled out of the driveway on my way to a meeting. A meeting for which I was now late and in no mood to participate. It was probably some meeting about being kind to your family. I wouldn't know. My mind was a blur the rest of the day.

And now it's 2:08 a.m. and I can't sleep.

I'm sad because of the way I acted today. I'm disappointed in my lack of self-control. I'm sad that I accused my girls when later I found the towels in my son's room. Go figure. And the more I relive my towel tirade, the more my brain refuses sleep.

I have to figure this out. What is my problem? Why can't I seem to control my reactions? I stuff. I explode. And I don't know how to get a handle on this. But God help me if I don't get a handle on this. I will destroy the relationships I value most and weave into my life permanent threads of short-temperedness, shame, fear, and frustration. Is that what I really want? Do I want my headstone to read, "Well, on the days she was nice she was really nice. But on the days she wasn't, rest assured, hell hath no fury like the woman who lies beneath the ground right here"?

No. That's not what I want. Not at all. I don't want the script of my life to be written that way. So, at 2:08 a.m., I vow to do better tomorrow. But better proves illusive, and my vow wears thin in the face of daily annoyances and other unpleasant realities. Tears slip and I'm worn out from trying. Always trying.

So who says emotions aren't bad? I feel like mine are. I feel broken. Unglued, actually. I have vowed to do better at 2:08 a.m. and 8:14 a.m. and 3:37 p.m. and 9:49 p.m. and many other minutes in between. I know what it's like to praise God one

> *I know what it's like to praise God one minute and in the next minute yell and scream at my child.*

minute and in the next minute yell and scream at my child—and then to feel both the burden of my destructive behavior and the shame of my powerlessness to stop it.

I also know what it's like to be on the receiving end of unglued behavior and to experience that painful sting of disrespect that makes me want to hurt the one who hurt me.

And the emotional demands keep on coming. Unrelenting insecurity. Wondering if anyone appreciates me. Feeling tired, stressed, hormonal.

Feeling unglued is really all I've ever known. And I'm starting to wonder if maybe it's all I'll ever be.

Those were the defeating thoughts I couldn't escape. Maybe you can relate. If you relate to my hurt, I pray you will also relate to my hope.

The Hope of Imperfect Progress

What kept me from making changes was the feeling that I wouldn't do it perfectly. I knew I'd still mess up and the changes wouldn't come instantly. Sometimes we girls think if we don't make instant progress, then real change isn't coming. But that's not so. There is a beautiful reality called *imperfect progress*. The day I realized the glorious hope of this kind of imperfect change is the day I gave myself permission to believe I really could be different.

Imperfect changes are slow steps of progress wrapped in grace . . . imperfect progress. And good heavens, I need lots of that. So, I dared to write this in my journal:

Progress. Just make progress. It's okay to have setbacks and the need for do-overs. It's okay to draw a line in the sand and start over again—and again. Just make sure you're moving the line forward. Move forward. Take baby steps, but at least take steps that keep you from being stuck. Then change will come. And it will be good.

These honest words enabled me to begin rewriting my story. Not that I erased what came before, but I stopped rehashing it and turned the page afresh. Eventually, I started blogging about my raw emotions and imperfect changes. In response, I got comments whispering, "Me too."

"Being unglued, for me, comes from a combination of anger and fear," wrote Kathy. "I think part of it is learned behavior. This is how my father was." Courtney honestly admitted, "I come unglued when I feel out of control because my kids are screaming or fighting or whining or negotiating and won't listen. I like silence, calm, obedience, and control. When it's not going 'my way,' I come unglued and freak out and it goes quiet. And then the regret comes."

Imperfect changes are slow steps of progress wrapped in grace ... imperfect progress.

And the comments kept coming, all of them expressing the exact same struggle, the same frustration, and the same need for hope. Women with kids and women without kids. Women caring for aging parents and women struggling with being the aging parent. Women working in the home and outside the home. So many women whose daily circumstances differed but whose core issues were the same.

I realized then that maybe other women could make some imperfect progress too. And this book was born from that simple realization. But I had to laugh at the irony of it. I had just published a book called *Made to Crave* that dealt with what goes into my mouth. Now I was writing a book called *Unglued* to deal with what comes out of my mouth.

Unglued is about my imperfect progress—a rewrite for the ongoing script of my life and a do-over of sorts for my raw emotions.

It's an honest admission that this struggle of reining in how I react has been hard for me. But hard doesn't mean impossible.

How hard something is often depends on your vantage point. For example, consider the shell of an egg. Looking at it from the outside, we know an eggshell is easily broken. But if you're looking at that same shell from the inside, it seems an impenetrable fortress. It's impossible for the raw white and tender yolk to penetrate the hardness of the eggshell. But given time and the proper incubation, the white and yolk develop into a new life that breaks through the shell and shakes itself free. And in the end, we can see that the hard work of cracking the shell was good for the new baby chick. The shell actually provided a place for new life to grow, and then enabled the chick to break forth in strength.

Might the same be true for *our* hard places? Might all this struggle with our raw emotions and unglued feelings have the exact same potential for new life and new strength?

I think so. I know so. I've seen so.

Indeed, emotions aren't bad.

The Promise of Progress

God gave us emotions. Emotions allow us to feel as we experience life. Because we feel, we connect. We share laughter and know the gift of empathy. Our emotions are what enable us to drink deeply from love and treasure it. And yes, we also experience difficult emotions such as sadness, fear, shame, and anger. But might these be important as well? Just as touching a hot stove signals our hand to pull back, might our hot emotions be alerting us to potential danger?

Yes, but I must remember God gave me emotions so I could experience life, not destroy it. There is a gentle discipline to it all. One I'm learning.

So, in the midst of my struggle and from the deep places of my heart, I scrawled out simple words about lessons learned, strategies discovered, Scriptures applied, imperfections understood, and grace embraced. I wrote about peace found, peace misplaced, flaws admitted, and forgiveness remembered. I celebrated progress made.

And that's the promise of this book. Progress. Nothing more. Nothing less. We won't seek instant change or quick fixes. We'll seek progress. Progress that will last long after the last page is turned.

We will walk through our progress together. You're not alone. Neither am I. Isn't that good to know? Isn't it good to have this little space and time together where it's okay to be vulnerable with what we've stuffed and to be honest about what we've spewed?

There will be tender mercies for the raw emotions. No need to bend under the weight of past mistakes. That kind of bending breaks us. And there has already been enough brokenness here. No, we won't bend from the weight of our past, but we will bow to the One who holds out hope for a better future. It's a truth-filled future in which God reveals how emotions can work for us instead of against us.

God gave me emotions so I could experience life, not destroy it.

Our progress is birthed in this truth, wrapped in the understanding that our emotions can work for us instead of against us. And then we get to cultivate that progress, nurture it, and watch it grow. Eventually, others will begin to see it and take notice. That's progress, lovely progress. Imperfect progress, but progress nonetheless.

Oh dear friend, there is a reason you are reading these words. There is a hurt we share. But might we also drink deeply from God's cup of hope and grace and peace as well? The fresh page is here for the turning. A new script is waiting to be written. And together we will be courageous women gathering up our unglued experiences and exchanging them for something new. New ways. New perspectives. New me. New you. And it will be good to make this imperfect progress together.

I'm Not a
Freak-out Woman

Sheer panic had me banging on the control, alt, and delete buttons simultaneously. "*Please!* No, no, no, no, no, no, no!" I turned off the computer, rebooted, and hoped beyond all reason that this little glitch was in fact little.

"Please work," I urgently whispered, hoping to appeal to the tender side of this machine I didn't have a clue how to fix.

My daughter had wanted to show me something really cool on the computer, so we snuggled up and waited for the website to load. Suddenly, a black warning box flashed up instead, covering most of my screen. You know it's not a good sign when your computer screen demands that you send $49.95 via your credit card to the Internet Security Program because you have been infected with something only they can fix. I knew it was a scam.

But I also knew whoever was behind it had no concern for me, the project due this Friday that was now locked inside this computer, or my suddenly raw and tangled emotions. Some evil computer masterminds with too much time on their hands and brains bent toward crime were holding my computer hostage. Everything I did to try to stop the virus just made it worse.

I picked up the phone to call my computer guy only to discover something had also messed with my phone. My entire contact list had been erased. What? I didn't even have my phone near the computer! How could both my phone and my computer go haywire at the same time?

My pulse raced. "You. Have. Got. To. Be. Kidding. Me!" I yelled while banging the side of my phone into my hand. Surely a little sideways jolt would reconnect whatever had gotten disconnected inside. Surely.

Then things got inexplicably worse. I suddenly felt like I was living out the lyrics of a bad country song when, in addition to all things technical going wrong, my dog started getting sick all over my bedroom carpet. Of course, it had to be the carpet. Ninety percent of the flooring downstairs is either wood or tile, which makes cleanup easy. But easy just wouldn't do in this moment.

Nope.

Surely one of my children would be eager to help me. But whining was the only response I got to my command for someone else to clean up after the dog so I could put an end to my technological Armageddon.

It was too much. Coming too fast. The perfect storm. And though I'd promised myself over and over and over I wouldn't explode, I did.

"Never, never, never will a child in this house ever be allowed to touch my computer! And if this dog throw-up isn't cleaned up by the time I walk back into my room, I'm giving the dog away!"

There would be no Proverbs 31-ish award given to me that night.

No kids to rise and call me blessed.

No husband bragging about me at the city gates.

No laughing at the days to come.

Indeed, nothing but tears and regret. Big, huge piles of regret. And dog throw-up. And a broken computer. And a psychotic cell phone.

I went to bed feeling like a cloud of yuck had wrapped itself around my head. There was no tidy ending to that day. No redeeming moment. No epiphany that rushed into my conscience and showed me how to fix it all. Just more stuff on my already overwhelming to-do list.

The next day I went to see one of those really smart computer guys, hoping to hear he could push one simple button and all would be well with my computer, my phone, and my dog. Call me Pollyanna.

In the end, he knew nothing about cell phones or dogs, and there would be no such thing as a one-button fix for my computer. The entire operating system on my laptop had been corrupted. However, he was able to retrieve most of what was stored on the hard drive. He downloaded it to an external hard drive, which he then copied over to a new computer. A new computer that cost me money I hadn't planned on spending.

I was relieved to have a working computer again but annoyed that all of this had happened in the first place. Until . . .

One month later my new computer was stolen. I know. Hard to believe, but oh so painfully true.

Tearfully, I called the same smart computer guy. Against all hope and reason, I wanted to know if he still had my old virus-corrupted computer so I could once again retrieve some data from the hard drive. He confirmed my fears — the computer had been trashed. But he also reminded me of the external hard drive he used for the transfer. I suddenly saw that original computer virus as one of the greatest things that had ever happened to me. It forced me to back up my entire computer on an external hard drive. This external hard drive was a great gift to have on the day when my new computer vanished. Had my computer never gotten that virus, I would never have taken the time to back up my computer. The virus that once seemed like a curse became a precious gift. Actually, it became a gift in more ways than one.

In that moment, I caught a glimpse of how crucial perspective is. In the midst of my latest computer tragedy, I stayed calm! It was a rare and empowering feeling. We'll talk a lot throughout this book about changing our perspective because perspective is a key to not coming unglued. For me, perspective doesn't just help me see the current circumstance I'm facing from a new vantage point—it also helps me process future things I face in a calmer, more grounded way. It helps me develop a new way of thinking. And this isn't just some theory I've observed in my life. It's actually the way God wired us.

Changing Our Thought Patterns

Brain research shows that every conscious thought we have is recorded on our internal hard drive known as the cerebral cortex. Each thought scratches the surface much like an Etch A Sketch. When we have the same thought again, the line of the original thought is deepened, causing what's called a memory trace. With each repetition the trace goes deeper and deeper, forming and embedding a pattern of thought. When an emotion is tied to this thought pattern, the memory trace grows exponentially stronger.

Renewing our minds with new thoughts is crucial. New thoughts come from new perspectives.

We forget most of our random thoughts that are not tied to an emotion. However, we retain the ones we think often that have an emotion tied to them. For example, if we've thought over and over that we are "unglued," and if that thought is tied to a strong emotion, we deepen the memory trace when we repeatedly access that thought. The same is true if we decide to stuff a thought—we'll perpetuate that stuffing. Or, if we yell, we'll keep yelling.

We won't develop new responses until we develop new thoughts. That's why renewing our minds with new thoughts is crucial. New thoughts come from new perspectives. The Bible encourages this process, which only makes sense because God created the human mind and understands better than anyone how it functions.

A foundational teaching of Scripture is that it is possible to be completely changed through transformed thought patterns:

> Do not conform to the pattern of this world, but be transformed by the renewing of your mind. Then you will be able to test and approve what God's will is — his good, pleasing and perfect will. (Romans 12:2)

Scripture also teaches that we can accept or refuse thoughts. Instead of being held hostage by old thought patterns, we can actually capture our thoughts and allow the power of Christ's truth to change them:

> We demolish arguments and every pretension that sets itself up against the knowledge of God, and we take captive every thought to make it obedient to Christ. (2 Corinthians 10:5)

I don't know about you, but understanding how my brain is designed makes these verses come alive in a whole new way for me. Taking thoughts captive and being transformed by thinking new ways isn't some New Age form of mind control. It's biblical and it's fitting with how God wired our brains. I can't control the things that happen to me each day, but I can control how I think about them. I can say to myself, "I have a choice to have destructive thoughts or constructive thoughts right now. I can wallow in what's wrong and make things worse, or I can ask God for a better perspective to help me *see* good even when I don't *feel* good." Indeed, when we gain new perspectives, we can see new ways of thinking.

Perspective taught me a valuable lesson through my computer debacle:

> *I can face things that are out of my control*
> *and not act out of control.*

Acting out of control only adds to my troubles. Gosh, I've done this time and time again. However, with the computer, I realized getting in a tizzy about it fixed nothing. It just added more stress and anxiety to an already tense situation. Yes, I can face things that are out of my control and not act out of control. This would be my new thought. This would be my new memory trace. This would be my new pattern.

I can face things that are out of my control and not act out of control.

But I couldn't just say it or think it. I had to believe it. And in order to believe it, I had to settle a matter of trust in my heart. *Could I trust God and believe that He is working out something good even from things that seem no good?* You see, if I know there is potential good hidden within each chaotic situation, I can loosen my grip on control.

It's easier to loosen my grip when I can see the good. When I can't immediately see the good, loosening my grip becomes a matter of trust. Either way, as I long as I believe—really believe—God is there and that He is out to do me good, I can stop freaking out trying to fix everything on my own. I can rest in the fact that God is in control. Which means I can face things that are out of my control and not act out of control.

Yes, this is a hard lesson to learn. But it's crucial.

Joshua's Question

Joshua had to learn how to deal with something out of his control without losing control when facing the impenetrable walls of Jericho. This is a pretty popular Bible story. But before you start skipping pages here thinking, "Been there, done that," wait! There's a little part of this story I hadn't discovered until recently. And I believe what happened to Joshua just before he gave his army their marching orders is one of the most significant lessons of the whole account.

It's a lesson wrapped up in a question Joshua asked. A question that reveals a great deal about Joshua's thought life — and a question we would be wise to ask ourselves. A crucial question. But before we get to the question, it's important to have a clear understanding of the context.

God instructed Joshua to lead the Israelites to capture the city of Jericho. But there was a problem. Jericho was protected by a massive wall that encircled the entire city.

I got a sense of what a walled-in city looks like when I visited the Vatican in Rome this summer. It was astounding. I stood at the base of this wall stretching several stories tall and thought of Joshua and what it must have felt like for him to stand at the wall of Jericho, which was higher still. And I felt the weight of the impossible.

If you were Joshua trying to formulate your battle plan, you'd see that Jericho itself was built on a hill, surrounded by an embankment, and encircled with a fifteen-foot stone retaining wall. On top of this retaining wall you'd see another mud brick wall that was six feet thick and twenty-five feet tall. That wall alone would be pretty intimidating, but it wasn't the only fortification you'd have to overcome. Surrounding this wall was yet another wall of similar size, approximately forty-five feet above ground level. Standing at the base of the outermost retaining wall, it would appear to you that the two walls together were over seventy feet tall. Without a doubt, this fortification would be impossible for the Israelites to overcome on their own.[1]

Think about looking at those walls, feeling the weight of the task before you, and knowing you will have to announce to your people a plan that in human reasoning makes absolutely no sense at all. Here is how the Bible describes it:

> Now Jericho was tightly shut up because of the Israelites. No one went out and no one came in. Then the LORD said to

Joshua, "See, I have delivered Jericho into your hands, along with its king and its fighting men. March around the city once with all the armed men. Do this for six days. Have seven priests carry trumpets of rams' horns in front of the ark. On the seventh day, march around the city seven times, with the priests blowing the trumpets. When you hear them sound a long blast on the trumpets, have all the people give a loud shout; then the wall of the city will collapse and the people will go up, every man straight in." (Joshua 6:1–5 NIV 1984)

That's it?

That's what he's going to tell the people whose forefathers had seen the walls and reported at Kadesh Barnea that the cities of Canaan were "large, with walls up to the sky" (Deuteronomy 1:28)?

Can you imagine the tweets, blog posts, and breaking news reports? Joshua is going to march around the city once a day for six days straight and then seven more times on the seventh day while toot-toot-tooting some horns. After marching and tooting, the people will shout and the walls — the huge, impossible, impenetrable walls of Jericho — will fall. Simply fall. The end.

If ever there were a moment for Joshua to feel overwhelmed at facing a situation totally out of his control, this would have been it. The plan was crazy. Short of a miraculous intervention from God, it wouldn't work. Joshua would be shamed. His people would be defeated. And to those who didn't believe, the God of Israel would be revealed as nothing more than a figment of Joshua's overactive imagination.

Talk about pressure.

But this is all part of the story with which you're probably familiar. Where's the little part that's less known? Less talked about? Less preached about? Where's the significant question I mentioned?

It's at the end of Joshua 5 when Joshua goes out to look at the walls before receiving his marching orders from the Lord.

There he is. And there the wall is.

Despite Joshua's long military experience, he had never led an attack on a fortified city that was so well prepared for a long siege. In fact, of all the walled cities in Canaan, Jericho was probably the most invincible. There was also the question of armaments. Israel's army had no siege engines, no battering rams, and no catapults. Their only weapons were slingshots, arrows, and spears — which were like straw toys against the walls of Jericho. Yet Joshua knew the battle of Jericho must be won because, having crossed the Jordan River, Israel's troops had no place to which they could retreat. Further, they could not bypass the city because that would leave their women, children, animals, and goods at Gilgal vulnerable to certain destruction.[2]

Pondering these heavy thoughts, Joshua is suddenly confronted by a man with a drawn sword. Scripture reveals that this is no mere human but "the commander of the army of the LORD" (Joshua 5:14) — God's presence in human form. Seeing that the man is ready for battle, Joshua asked, "Are you for us or for our enemies?" (Joshua 5:13).

Wrapped in this question we see a hesitancy in Joshua — a peek inside his thought life — a need for reassurance. Such an honest question, but one that makes me feel Joshua isn't walking in complete confidence and assurance. If he were, he wouldn't have asked. But he did. And this is where we assume that, of course God's presence will answer, "Joshua, I am with you, for you, and on your side!"

But we would assume wrong.

When asked, "Are you for us or for our enemies?" the presence of God says, "Neither."

Why?

Because Joshua has asked the wrong question of the wrong person. The question that needed to be asked and answered wasn't whose side God was on. The real question was one Joshua should have asked himself:

"Whose side am *I* on?"

The same goes for us. When faced with a situation out of our control, we need to ask, "Whose side am I on?" Will our response reflect that we are on God's side or not? If we determine that, no matter what, we're on God's side, it settles the trust issue in our hearts. And if we ground ourselves in the reality that we trust God, we can face circumstances that are out of our control without acting out of control. We can't always fix our circumstances, but we can fix our minds on God. We can do that.

We can't always fix our circumstances, but we can fix our minds on God.

Joshua did it.

> The seven priests carrying the seven trumpets went forward, marching before the ark of the LORD and blowing the trumpets. The armed men went ahead of them and the rear guard followed the ark of the LORD, while the trumpets kept sounding. So on the second day they marched around the city once and returned to the camp. They did this for six days. On the seventh day, they got up at daybreak and marched around the city seven times in the same manner, except that on that day they circled the city seven times. The seventh time around, when the priests sounded the trumpet blast, Joshua commanded the people, "Shout! For the LORD has given you the city!" (Joshua 6:13–16 NIV 1984)

With that, the walls of Jericho came crashing down. They were impossible no more.

I like the thought of *impossible* being erased from my vocabulary. Especially when it comes to my struggles with feeling unglued. I am on God's side. I can reflect that in my actions and reactions. I can face things out of my control without acting out of control.

One Good Choice

That night while I was waiting for the smart computer guy to upload my external hard drive onto another laptop, my daughter Ashley and I ran across the street to the mall. The mall—with all the crowds and chaotic pull of store after store trying to get me to buy, buy, buy—isn't my favorite place. But in the midst of it all, my daughter looked up at me and said, "You know what I really like about you? You're not a freak-out woman when bad things happen."

I wanted to cry.

Because the reality is I have been a freak-out woman way too many times. And I hate that. But somehow, the one good choice not to freak out about my computer being stolen transformed my daughter's perception. It redefined my trajectory. One good choice. Imperfect progress.

If it took sacrificing my laptop to have that one experience with Ashley, I would gladly give up my computer all over again. (Note to Jesus: *I'm certainly not suggesting that. Honestly, I think I have learned this lesson and have no need to replace my computer again for a good long while.*)

I can face things that are out of my control and not act out of control.

I am not a freak-out woman.

Am I on God's side or Satan's?

Satan	God
Control	Peace
Panic	Patience
Anger	Gentleness
Manipulation	Self Control
"God Beat"	Trust

The Prisoners

The courtroom hushed as the judge prepared to read the sentence. All the hoping-praying-waiting-wishing we could change things, all the begging for mercy, had led to this. This moment. The words on this paper. The sentence for my friend, Christina.

My heart drummed wildly as I stared ahead. All I could see was the back of her head, sitting atop a frame hunched painfully small. Christina stood. And the judge opened his mouth to speak.

Three years earlier, Christina and I had spent hours together scouring discount stores for pictures and knick-knacks with which to decorate my home. Making homes beautiful on a budget was Christina's art form. She was a master at spotting a treasure on a shelf full of broken, picked-over, deeply discounted things. She somehow saw potential in these discards that completely eluded me.

She could visualize rescued treasures as things of beauty when taken off the discount shelf and put in a different space—a shelf in my den, a corner in my kitchen, on my nightstand. "Trust me," she'd say, "it will be beautiful. You'll see." Because that's what makes an artist: the ability to see beyond what *is* to what *can be*.

"Oh God," I said under my breath, "please let Christina be

able to do that now—to see beyond what is to what can be." Tears washed down my face as the judge told her she'd be going to prison.

Prison.

The word fell hard. Christina had three months to make arrangements for her family and then life as she knew it would end for at least a year. Maybe more.

Christina had gotten caught up in a real estate scheme she neither created nor fully understood. But she took full responsibility for her mistakes and would now pay a steep price: her freedom. This precious friend, a beautiful mother of two young kids, an artist with delightful taste, was about to become a prison number.

I walked away from the courtroom that day trying to think of words to comfort Christina. There were none. What she had done was wrong. I got that. She got that. And we all knew there would be consequences—there *should* be consequences. But it still didn't stop my heart from feeling completely undone at the thought of Christina going to prison.

A prisoner. This label states so much. And I didn't want that "so much" to forever define my friend. Might this woman, who always saw beauty in the broken, discarded things of the world, somehow see beauty hidden in her own life? Might I one day hear her say once again, "Trust me, it will be beautiful. You'll see"?

Could *I* see broken to beautiful for her, even in this?

Or would this part of her life forever define her, label her as the woman who'd gone to prison?

Labels

Labels are awful. They imprison us in categories that are hard to escape. I should know. While I've never been a numbered inmate in a federal prison, I've put labels on myself that have certainly locked me into hard places. Maybe you are familiar with labels too . . .

I am angry.

I am frustrated.

I am a screamer.

I am a stuffer.

I am just like my mother.

I am a wreck.

I am a people pleaser.

I am a jerk.

I am insecure.

I am unglued.

And the list goes on.

Well, I learned a powerful lesson about labels in a quite unexpected place— a children's book. Which is just hilarious because (don't tell my kids) I am the queen of skipping pages in children's books and making up my own story. Tired mamas do these things. So the fact that I actually read this one word for word is really amazing.

Max Lucado's *You Are Special* is fantastic. Perhaps you've read it too. The main character, Punchinello, is one of the Wemmicks, a small wooden people who spend their days sticking gray dots or gold stars on each other. Punchinello struggles to deal with the negative labels —the ugly, gray dots—that other Wemmicks have stuck to him. The "aha" moment in the story comes when someone tells Punchinello, "The dots only stick if you let them."

> *Labels are awful. They imprison us in categories that are hard to escape.*

I know the story is for kids, but I must say these words were an epiphany for me even as an adult. *Labels only stick if I let them.* That was a complete revelation, especially in connection with the labels I put on myself. Those labels start out as little threads of self-dissatisfaction but ultimately weave together into a straitjacket of self-condemnation.

When I thought about the ugly label Christina might carry with her throughout her life, I realized she wasn't the only prisoner in the courtroom that day. I was an inmate in a prison of my own design, locked behind the many, many labels I'd put on myself over the years. I'd resigned myself to the lie that I would forever be enslaved to my emotions. And I spoke to myself in ways I'd never let another person speak to me:

> You're so __emotional__
> You always __"lose it"__.
> Things will never get better. You're just __too sensitive__

I filled in all the blanks with self-condemning labels that tore me down.

Take my struggle with organization. For months, my messy closet was a source of mental contention. Every day I walked in and out of this space thinking, *Uggghhhh! Why am I so disorganized? Why can't I have a closet like so-and-so? I don't think she ever struggles with keeping things tidy. I'm just a mess.*

I labeled myself as a mess and then resigned myself to forever being a mess.

I did the same thing with my family's tendency to run late. I hate to run late, and yet the realities of getting five kids anywhere on time is quite the challenge. But instead of rising to the challenge and putting parameters in place to ensure on-time departures, I just felt defeated. *I'm late and I'm always going to be late. Why even try to be on time?* I labeled myself as a late person and resigned myself to forever running late.

A soul who believes she can't leave ... doesn't.

Trapped inside these straitjacket struggles was a girl dying to break free from all the self-defeating labels. Some prisons don't require bars to keep people locked inside. All it takes is their perception that they belong there. A soul who believes she can't leave ... doesn't.

But what is a girl to do?

We know we have issues, and labeling ourselves is what comes naturally to us—it's just what we do. How we act is how we label ourselves. We don't know any other way.

I didn't know any other way ... until I saw another way.

The Unfinished Sculpture

Again, it was an unexpected place. Just as I don't often read children's books word for word, I don't often visit museums either. However, I'd read some fascinating facts about the *David* by Michelangelo and made it my mission to go and see the original at the Accademia Gallery in Florence, Italy.

A two-hour wait in a long line of tourists gave me plenty of time to read the museum brochure about the *David* sculpture. To my surprise, I discovered that Michelangelo wasn't the artist who began the sculpture—in fact, he hadn't even been born when it was commissioned. The nineteen-foot block of marble had originally been the project of an artist named Agostino di Duccio, but after shaping some of the legs, feet, and torso, he inexplicably abandoned the work. Ten years later, an artist named Antonio Rossellino was hired to complete it, but his contract was subsequently cancelled. It was nearly twenty-five years before Michelangelo, just twenty-six, picked up a chisel and dared to believe he could complete a masterpiece.

Sources say the artist never left his *David*. For more than two years he worked on and slept beside the six-ton slab of marble whose subject called to him from inside the unchiseled places. When at last the seventeen-foot *David* emerged, Michelangelo is reported to have said, "I saw the angel in the marble and carved until I set him free." When asked how he made his statue, Michelangelo is reported to have said, "It is easy. You just chip away the stone that doesn't look like David."

And now I was about to see it for myself—this sculpture finished in 1504 that many have called an artistic miracle. I stopped just inside the narrow main corridor, still thirty feet from the *David*. This was not where everyone else wanted to stop and so I caused a bit of a traffic jam. We had been waiting outside in the hot sun and now that we were finally inside, everyone was on a mission.

Indeed, I understood why everyone rushed past me. Why would anyone stop to stare at what captivated me—the much less impressive unfinished sculptures lining the hallway? Why attend to blocks of stone with roughly hewn, half-completed figures when sculpted perfection stands just a short walk away? Who would stop? Who would even care to notice?

A woman captivated by seeing her interior reality vividly depicted in stone, that's who. I stood in the shadow of one of the unfinished sculptures that's part of this collection aptly titled, *Prisoners*. And I stared.

I tilted my head and let it soak in. I didn't want this experience to be a gentle breeze that passed through me and was quickly forgotten. I wanted it to be a rush of mighty wind, not enough to take me down but enough to rip loose the labels wrapped so tightly around my soul. I felt it way down deep. This less-noticed sculpture was me—an unfinished prisoner locked away in a hard place, labeled and on prominent display in a hallway leading to greatness.

Oh God, chisel me. I don't want to be locked in my hard places forever.

Then I turned and looked down the corridor at the *David*, the statue fully chiseled by a master artist. And as I walked toward it, I whispered, "O God, chisel me. I don't want to be locked in my hard places forever. I want to be free. I want to be all that You have in mind for me to be."

In that moment, I recognized a truth I'd needed to see for a long, long time: *It is beautiful when the Master chisels*. God doesn't allow the unglued moments of our lives to happen so we'll label ourselves and stay stuck. He allows the unglued moments to make us aware of the chiseling that needs to be done. So instead of condemning myself with statements like, *I'm such a mess*, I could say, *Let God chisel. Let Him work on my hard places so I can leave the dark places of being stuck and come into the light of who He designed me to be.* God is calling us out—out of darkness, out from those places we thought would never get better, out of being stuck.

Refuse the Labels of the Past

One of my favorite passages that confirms God calling us out of the darkness is from 1 Peter:

> As you come to him, the living Stone—rejected by [humans] but chosen by God and precious to him   you also, like living stones, are being built into a spiritual house to be a holy priesthood, offering spiritual sacrifices acceptable to God through Jesus Christ ... you are a chosen people, a royal priesthood, a holy nation, a people belonging to God, that you may declare the praises of him who called you out of darkness into his wonderful light. (1 Peter 2:4–5, 9 NIV 1984)

These words were penned by the apostle Peter. The name Peter means "the rock," but Peter's given name was Simon, which means "shifty." I can't escape the richness of meaning here that Peter "the rock" didn't get stuck being shifty his whole life. He let God chisel. Remember, Peter was the one who dared to jump out of the boat and walk on water. Then he got afraid, started to sink, and cried out to the Lord to save him. In a matter of moments, he went from being bold to being scolded for his doubt (Matthew 14:22–32).

Peter was also the man who loved his Lord with such passion that he drew his sword and cut off the ear of the guard trying to arrest Jesus (John 18:10). Then, just seven short verses later, we find this same Peter denying he even knew Jesus: "You are not one of [the] disciples, are you?" the girl at the door asked Peter. He replied, "I am not" (John 18:17 NIV 1984).

He sure sounds shifty to me.

But not to Jesus. Jesus saw a courageous man who needed chiseling. Jesus saw a man who, when chiseled, would boldly do what others would not. Jesus saw Peter not as he was but as he could be.

Tenderly, Jesus chiseled. After Peter denied Jesus, and Jesus was crucified and resurrected, Peter and Jesus had a conversation in which we get to see Jesus chiseling. Three times Peter denied Jesus. Three times Jesus asked if Peter loved Him. I can almost hear the Master's chisel clink and chip and smooth.

> When they had finished eating, Jesus said to Simon Peter, "Simon son of John, do you truly love me more than these?"
>
> "Yes, Lord," he said, "you know that I love you."
>
> Jesus said, "Feed my lambs."
>
> Again Jesus said, "Simon son of John, do you truly love me?"
>
> He answered, "Yes, Lord, you know that I love you."
>
> Jesus said, "Take care of my sheep."
>
> The third time he said to him, "Simon son of John, do you love me?"
>
> Peter was hurt because Jesus asked him the third time, "Do you love me?" He said, "Lord, you know all things; you know that I love you." (John 21:15–17 NIV 1984)

Later, in Acts, we see evidence of the chiseled Peter. He's bold, assured, prepared to do the work the Master created him to do:

> Then Peter stood up with the Eleven, raised his voice and addressed the crowd: "Fellow Jews and all of you who live in Jerusalem, let me explain this to you; listen carefully to what I say." … With many other words he warned them; and he pleaded with them, "Save yourselves from this corrupt generation." Those who accepted his message were baptized, and

about three thousand were added to their number that day. (Acts 2:14, 40–41)

He doesn't sound like shifty Simon to me anymore. He is Peter, chiseled Peter, whose bold preaching led three thousand people to dedicate their lives to Christ and be baptized—in one day!

The apostle Paul is another man who refused the label of his past. Saul, the persecutor of Christians, became Paul, the writer of much of the New Testament! He wrote in his letter to the Ephesians, "For we are God's workmanship, created in Christ Jesus to do good works, which God prepared in advance for us to do" (Ephesians 2:10 NIV 1984).

Paul was God's workmanship. Peter was God's workmanship. We are God's workmanship! God is chiseling us, making us new, releasing us from our hard places—those places that make us feel so stinkin' defeated—so we can do good works. Works God has *prepared for us*, which means He knows best how to *prepare in us* the character we need to fulfill our calling.

Oh that we might hear the purposeful clink of the Master's chisel and call it grace:

> For it is by grace you have been saved, through faith—and this not from yourselves, it is the gift of God—not by works, so that no one can boast. For we are God's workmanship, created in Christ Jesus to do good works, which God prepared in advance for us to do. (Ephesians 2:8–10 NIV 1984)

Is it true? Will I see grace and feel grace and call it grace when I come unglued? Even when, like Peter, I deny Christ with my actions? When, like Paul, I have a past that's anything but godly? Will I embrace the grace by which I've been saved through faith—choose to see myself as God's workmanship—and do the good work I've been called to?

Call It Grace

Are you ready to see yourself as God's workmanship and do the work you've been called to do? Let me share how I practically did this. Remember the messy closet that led me to define myself as a mess? Then when I defined myself as a mess, my emotions felt even messier. I was more short-tempered and off-kilter. As I untangled the root of what was making me feel this way, I did three things:

1. I identified the label as a lie meant to tear me down.

The reality: My closet was messy. The lie: A messy closet means I am a mess. The truth: A messy closet does not make me a mess. It makes me a child of God who has a messy closet.

Grace. I can see it. I can feel it. I can call it grace.

2. I chose to view this circumstance as a call to action, not a call to beat myself up mentally.

A messy closet means I need to hit the pause button on life one day and clean it. And if I can't figure out how to clean it, then I need to find someone gifted in this area to help me. And that's exactly what I did. My friend Lisa has the spiritual gift of closet organization. (Is there such a thing??) I saved up my pennies and paid her to come and share some of that Jesus-equipping with me.

> *A messy closet does not make me a mess. It makes me a child of God who has a messy closet.*

Grace. I can see it. I can feel it. I can call it grace.

3. I used the momentum of tackling one label to help me tackle more.

Taking action and tearing down this one label in my life has given me the courage to tackle other labels. Oh, the courage and strength found in starting somewhere! Might you find a small label to tackle today?

Grace. You will see it. You will feel it. You will call it grace.

Christina came to understand the power of grace in prison. After being incarcerated several months, Christina wrote, "Lysa, I am doing really well! I am so hungry for God's Word, and God is really using me to pray and share the gospel with other women here. The absolute terror I felt about coming to prison has been surrendered to God, and in place of that old fear is a strength, peace, and hope for the future. God revealed why I *had* to come here! He's led me to repent for things I hadn't even realized held me in bondage for so many years." *divorce did the same for me!*

Grace. A woman goes to prison and finds freedom from her real bondage.

My mind went back to the hush of the courtroom that day. To the comforting words I wanted to say but couldn't find. To my tears and questions and fear that Christina would forever be labeled as a prisoner. Now I see God's workmanship even in this hard chiseling Christina is experiencing. Christina made the choices that put her in prison, but it was God who freed her in the midst of that place.

Let God chisel. "Trust me," God says, "it will be beautiful. You'll see."

Grace. She sees it. She feels it. And now, even in prison, she still calls it grace.

I'm not a poem girl, but every now and then I stumble across one that captures the essence of what God has been teaching me. My friend Genia saw the following in her daily devotional, *Streams in the Desert*, and knew she had to send it my way:

> *In the still air the music lies unheard;*
> *In the rough marble beauty hides unseen;*
> *To make the music and the beauty needs*
> *The master's touch, the sculptor's chisel keen.*
> *Great Master, touch us with Your skillful hands;*

Let not the music that is in us die!
Great Sculptor, hew and polish us; nor let,
Hidden and lost, Your form within us lie! [3]

Indeed, Master, touch us with Your sculptor's chisel keen.

And with that, we continue our journey toward imperfect progress. I don't know what labels you've been struggling with or struggling through but, friend, let's unglue them. In that sense, I rather like the thought of being an *unglued woman*.

Labels

- I never finish anything
- I am easily distracted
- I can't stay focused
- I can't say "no" to anyone.

Breaking the label —
I can be pleasant and still not take the monkey on my back. I can remain focused on my goals, which will in turn help me "finish" things on my list.

4

What Kind
of Unglued Am I?

Am I an exploder? Or am I a stuffer?

I knew I needed to answer these questions in order to really face up to my raw emotions. Emotions don't sit still. They are active —and they travel. I needed to know where mine were taking me so I could understand why I sometimes came unglued.

As I wrestled with the exploder or stuffer question, I realized I was having a hard time defining myself. I needed to define myself not for the purpose of labeling, but for identifying, for naming what is true. There is a big difference between labeling ourselves and identifying our tendencies. Labeling says, "I am a sum total of my difficult issues." We've already discussed in the previous chapter why this isn't healthy or productive.

Identifying, on the other hand, says, "My issues are part of the equation but not the sum total." It's both healthy and productive to identify the issues that cause us to react badly when we are stressed, irritated by people who get on our nerves, stuck in conflicts, feeling hurt or causing hurt, at the mercy of raging hormones, or drenched in our raw emotions.

This identification process seemed simple enough on first glance:

43

people come unglued and react in one of two ways, either by exploding or by stuffing.

Exploding means pushing emotions outward. A rush of feelings surge up and out of our mouths and bring a whole host of lovelies along with them—stern words, harsh looks, raised voices, condemning attitudes, and demonstrative gestures such as slamming doors or banging our hands down on a table. But rest assured: there are quiet exploders too; we don't have to be loud to hurt another person just as swiftly and directly. Indeed, the telltale sign of being an exploder is not the decibel level but having reactions that feel good *in the moment* because it gets the yuck out. But when we realize how we've spewed on others and the hurt we've caused, the regret falls heavy.

> *The telltale sign of being an exploder is not the decibel level.*

Yes, we regret exploding. But we'll either deflect that regret by blaming someone else for our actions or we'll ingest that regret by shaming ourselves. Either way, exploding feels good in the short term but awful in the long term.

Stuffing means pushing emotions inward. We swallow hard and lock our hurt feelings inside, not in an effort to process and release them, but to wallow in the hurt. Much like an oyster deals with the irritation of a grain of sand, we coat the issue with more and more layers of hurt until it forms a hard rock of sorts.

But this rock is no pearl. It's a rock that we'll eventually use either to build a barrier or to hurl at someone else in retaliation.

So, after pondering these definitions, studying thousands of responses to blog posts I've written on raw emotions, and honestly assessing myself, I determined there are not two but four categories of unglued reactions I needed to pay attention to:

Exploders who shame themselves

Exploders who blame others

Stuffers who build barriers

Stuffers who collect retaliation rocks

Can you see yourself in any of these? I can. Just writing them down on paper started to bring clarity to the topic.

Four Categories of Unglued Reactions

After identifying the four categories, I wanted to know which one I fall into. Now, here's where things got really interesting.

I realized I fall into all four categories!

Depending on the situation and the people involved, I shift my unglued reactions. I know I will pay a cost for coming unglued. Somehow, I instinctively measure this cost and decide with whom and in what circumstances I can afford to either explode and let it all rip or stuff it and pretend nothing's wrong.

I'm not proud of this, nor am I saying any of these behaviors is good. But for a minute, might I step out of my role as a Christian speaker and author and just be your gut-honest friend? For the sake of my own soul, it's important for me to lay it all on the table. So, I'm splitting my heart wide open and being as raw as it gets right here. I'm going to explain each of these categories, not from a removed clinical viewpoint, but from honest admissions from my own life. In this chapter I'll paint a clear picture of the four reactions and in the next two chapters we'll talk about how to make imperfect progress with each. Heavens, it's about to get a little messy around here ... but I know you'll understand and that's why I love you so.

The Exploder Who Shames Herself

When I'm feeling unglued with a stranger, I tend to be an exploder who later shames herself for not being more Christian-like.

My unglued reaction with this stranger probably won't be loud or draw the attention of others. That doesn't really fit my personality. But if someone is rude, disrespectful, or belligerent, I can certainly have a stern reaction. It might be quietly stern, but this person will have no doubt I'm unhappy. As I said earlier, exploders aren't always loud in conveying their point, but they do use their words and tone to make sure the other person *feels* their point.

When an airline recently lost my friend Holly's luggage, I was elected to go to the lost luggage office and see what could be done. The woman behind the counter saw me coming and held her hand up with a quick and cutting, "Don't even come in here until you've looked through the pile to the left."

So much for flying the friendly skies. I dutifully looked through the pile of homeless luggage, and there wasn't one suitcase that looked anything like Holly's. So, I proceeded to walk toward the office again.

"You didn't look!" yelled the woman behind the counter. "I told you to look *through* that pile."

I swallowed. Hard.

"I did look and I can guarantee you the piece of luggage I'm looking for isn't there," I said.

She rolled her eyes, motioned for me to approach her desk, and continued to do everything in her power to act as if losing Holly's suitcase was somehow my fault. I dealt with it. And dealt with it. And then got tired of dealing with it.

"Look," I snapped, "I am the customer here. Your airline lost our luggage. I wish I didn't have to be in this little office right now. But I am because it is *your job* to help me. And that's exactly what I need you to do . . . your job."

I didn't raise my voice. But I did raise my intensity. I let the situation dictate my reaction, and I walked away feeling frustrated but justified. Until an hour later. I had this nagging sense I'd blown it. I started thinking of several of my gentle friends who never would have talked sharply or gotten caught up in their frustration: *Amy wouldn't have acted that way. Samantha would have used this as a golden opportunity to love the unlovely. Ann would have given so much grace, a revival would have taken place right there in the lost luggage office, and years later this lady would be sharing her testimony of how everything changed the day that kind woman came to her office.*

Ugh. Shame slithered up close and whispered, "Look at you and all your Bible studying ... what good is it all? What good are you?" The heaviness in my soul left me with this sinking feeling that I wouldn't ever really be able to change. And a familiar thought ran through a well-worn rut in my brain: *I'll probably always be a slave to the raw emotions that catch me off guard.*

What a lie.

If you've been believing this same lie, hang on to this truth: Just the fact that you're reading this book is a sign of great progress. Refuse to wallow in the depressing angst condemnation brings. On the other hand, embrace any conviction you feel. Condemnation defeats us. Conviction unlocks the greatest potential for change.

The Exploder Who Blames Others

When I'm feeling unglued with my kids, I tend to be an exploder who blames them for pushing me to this place.

I can wake up in the best mood, determined to have a shine-my-mommy halo day, only to have that halo slip into a noose around my neck minutes later. Ever been there? Well, here is just a snapshot of one of those days when five kids lead one mom to feel more than slightly unglued ...

I told the younger kids to put on their shoes but, of course, when it's time to go and I grab the keys, everyone still has bare feet. Meanwhile, my son has put a biscuit wrapped in tinfoil in the microwave, and the smell coming from the kitchen is so completely toxic I can no longer breathe. Not to mention that when I open the microwave door, I discover that the plastic interior has melted in on itself.

My other son needs ten dollars for some club T-shirt, and he's three days late turning in the money. Every other kid turned in their money early. As I'm digging through my purse whispering to myself, *Please help me find ten dollars. Please, oh please, let there be ten dollars in my purse,* I'm suddenly confronted with an even bigger concern. *My heavens, where is my wallet? Forget the ten dollars! Oh my gracious, where in the world did I leave my wallet?!*

The missing-shoes kids start crying. The melted-microwave boy starts complaining that *my* microwave ruined *his* breakfast. And if the ten-dollar boy tells me one more time he needs money, I'm going tell him to stick that money where the sun don't shine. Doesn't shine. Whatever. And now my wallet is missing.

We are *that* family. I imagine our name written in huge red letters hanging on the front of the school: "The TerKeursts are a mess. They are late. They wear mismatched shoes. And they smell toxic. Beware!"

Beware indeed.

By the time we all make it to the car to start getting everyone where they need to go, I've had it.

"If you people would put your shoes on when I tell you to, and listen when I remind you for the hundredth time not to put foil in the microwave — *ever, ever, ever* — and warn me in advance when you need money, and give me just a minute during my day to focus so I don't lose my wallet and therefore feel like I'm going to lose my mind (inhale), we'd all be *much better off!* But *no, no, no.* None of that is possible because we are *that* family — crazy and chaotic and completely a mess!"

I try to throw out a quick, "But I love you," as they get out of the car and head into school. My sentiments fall flat. I blame them for all the chaos that's gotten us to this unglued place. And later the regret of it all falls heavy. So heavy.

I get that sinking feeling again that I won't ever really be able to change: *I'll probably always be a slave to the raw emotions that catch me off guard.*

What a lie.

The Stuffer Who Builds Barriers

When I'm feeling unglued with my friends or my parents, I tend to be a stuffer who builds barriers.

I was on the phone with a friend talking through a situation regarding two of our kids. They'd gotten into a little tiff about something. I don't even remember now what the issue was, but I certainly remember why it escalated into something that led me to determine our friendship was no longer safe.

We had what I thought was a great discussion about how to help our kids manage the issue at hand. We came up with a plan of what she was going to address with her child and what I was going to address with mine. We ended the call on a great note.

A few hours later, she called back. I missed the call so my phone rolled over to voice mail. She left a quick message about how the talk went with her child and thought she'd disconnected the call. But the call was still very much active, and my voice mail then recorded her tirade about me, my children, and my family in general.

I was stunned. Beyond stunned.

I stared into the sky and wished I could become as weightless as a cloud and float away. "I can't deal with this," I reasoned. "I don't know what to say or how to say it." So I said nothing. Not a word. I stuffed it all down and started to build a barrier to hide behind. After the

"Everything's fine," I said. But everything wasn't fine.

incident, I smiled when I saw her, but I held her at a distance. She knew something was wrong, but when she questioned me about it, I lied.

"Everything's fine," I said. But everything wasn't fine. Not at all.

As the communication died, so did the relationship. The regret fell heavy. So heavy. And there it was again. That sinking feeling I wouldn't ever really be able to change: *I'll probably always be a slave to the raw emotions that catch me off guard.*

What a lie.

The Stuffer Who Collects Retaliation Rocks

When I'm feeling unglued with my husband, I tend to collect retaliation rocks to use as weapons in future disagreements.

When Art and I were dating, I picked up on the fact that he loved to exercise. It didn't take a rocket scientist to quickly discern that I could spend more time with him if I suddenly developed a passion for exercising too. And oh, how I longed to do just that. So I started running. I'd never been able to run before, but the giddy-in-love feelings of a serious crush enabled me to push past the pain and keep in step with my man.

An important fact to note here: I loved him. I loved spending time with him. I did not, however, love running. So, when we got married and we had all the time in the world together, I no longer wanted to run. At all.

Art was baffled by my bait and switch. I was annoyed that he made such a big deal about still wanting us to run together. As I made excuses each time he asked me to run, I kept the peace by smiling, all the while swallowing little gulps of bitterness. *He should love me whether or not I run with him.* Smile and swallow. *He shouldn't keep asking me.* Smile and swallow. *He's making me feel like his love is conditional.* Smile and swallow. *Oh dear, is his love conditional? If so, we have marriage problems.* Smile and swallow. *I think we do have marriage problems.* And on and on went the smile-and-swallow routine.

Each time I smiled and swallowed, I formed little bitter rocks that sat heavy in my soul, waiting for just the right moment to pull them out and retaliate with all this proof of how much he was damaging our marriage.

What started as an annoyance developed over the years into a long-term issue that would erupt each time I felt pricked by this thought of "conditional love." One of these "pricks" happened on the day he brought me lunch. I was under some tight deadlines, and since he owns a Chick-fil-A, he offered to bring me some of my favorite chicken in the world. I ordered a sandwich with a Coke. A regular Coke.

But what he brought me was a sandwich with a Diet Coke.

When I saw the little diet button depressed on the lid of the cup, all the insecurity and resentment I'd stuffed shot up from a dark corner within, and I pummeled him with retaliation rocks.

"You think I'm fat!" and here's the rock that proves it. "You think I'm lazy!" and here's the rock that proves it. "You wish I were different!" and here's the rock that proves it. "You wish you'd never married me!" and here's the rock that proves it. *Wham! Wham! Wham! Wham!*

All over a Diet Coke. A Diet Coke that he was kind to bring me. Good gracious. The regret eventually fell heavy once again. So heavy.

Yes, like I said before, it's the same sinking feeling that I won't ever really be able to change: *I'll probably always be a slave to the raw emotions that catch me off guard — a slave locked in the hard places.*

What a lie.

Soul Integrity

All these reactions I've described are not things I'm proud of. Yuck, right? Yes, but these aren't labels I carry around with me. These are things I'm identifying about myself so I can bring my raw emotions and unglued reactions under the healing authority of Jesus.

And it's also important to clarify that I'm only talking about my unglued reactions here. When my emotions are level, I am like the little girl in that movie, *The Help*, to whom the beloved Aibileen leans down and whispers, "You is kind. You is smart. You is important."

Jesus has made me a **kind**-hearted person, full of encouragement and eager to inspire any person who gets within ten feet of me. Jesus has made me **smart** enough to know that I need Him—desperately and fully. And Jesus has assigned all of us the **important** job of representing Him to this world, which means we re-present Him everywhere we go.

Yes, kind, smart, important—that's who I am. And that's how I act and react a lot of the time. But not all the time. Especially not when I feel unglued and the integrity of my soul unravels.

Soul integrity is honesty that's godly. It brings the passion of the exploder and the peacemaking of the stuffer under the authority of Jesus.

In processing unglued reactions, soul integrity is the heart of what we're after. Soul integrity is honesty that's godly. It brings the passion of the exploder and the peacemaking of the stuffer under the authority of Jesus where honesty and godliness embrace and balance each other.

When I explode, I embrace the honesty part but refuse to be reined in by the godly part. You see, my honest feelings may not be truthful assessments of the situation. I can be honest with how I feel and still exaggerate or misinterpret what is factually true. I can feel justified in being blatant about my feelings—not hiding a thing—and prideful for being so *real*, all under the guise of being honest enough not to stuff. But in reality, honesty that isn't true isn't honesty at all. It may just be emotional spewing. That's why we need *godly* honesty—honesty reined in by the Holy Spirit—if we're going to have authentic soul integrity.

In the Christian world we often excuse this kind of unbalanced honesty with little justifications such as, "I'm just keeping it real," "I'm just sayin'," "I'm just being honest," "Sometimes the truth hurts."

Oh, how it must grieve God's heart to see His people reject the godliness that should always balance out our honesty. How it must sadden God to see me do this. And you. And our friends. And our ministry coworkers. And the leaders of the church. And the people in our church. Yes, it's all of us at times.

At the same time, it must also grieve God to see plastic versions of godliness that aren't reined in by honesty. That's what we do when we stuff and pretend everything is okay. The upside of stuffing is that we have the semblance of peacemakers. But when we do this at the expense of honesty, we harbor a corrosive bitterness that will eventually emerge. Either it will erode our health and later present itself in a host of emotional and physical anxiety-induced illnesses, or it will accumulate over time and surprise everyone when the peacemaker eventually erupts.

Saying "I'm fine" to keep the peace, when we're really not fine, isn't honest. It may seem godly in the moment, but it's false godliness. Truth and godliness always walk hand in hand. The minute we divorce one from the other, we stray from soul integrity and give a foothold to the instability that inevitably leads to coming unglued.

Let me explain how soul integrity could have played out in one of the unglued stories I've already shared. I could have called the friend who inadvertently spewed on my voicemail. Knowing that I couldn't control how she acts and reacts, I still could have controlled how

I acted and reacted by gently telling her what I heard and asking her to help me understand. I could have extended her forgiveness while simultaneously being honest about my hurt.

I'm not saying this would have saved our relationship. Just because we extend forgiveness doesn't mean we keep that person in our close-knit circle. Forgiveness is mandatory; reconciliation is optional. However, I do think it would have opened the lines of communication and saved me from months of inner turmoil. It would have saved her the confusion of sensing the barrier between us while I simultaneously denied that anything was wrong. We might both have grown and matured as a result, possibly even ironing out some issues and reclaiming our friendship. I don't know what I missed out on, but I am determined to practice soul integrity moving forward. So much of pursuing this soul integrity means carefully watching our words.

Listen to the Bible's warning about how we use words:

> People can tame all kinds of animals, birds, reptiles, and fish,
> but no one can tame the tongue. It is restless and evil, full of
> deadly poison. (James 3:7–8 NLT)

In other words, we must bring all of our raw reactions under the authority and truth of Jesus. Our best efforts at human reasoning and willpower can't tame what we say externally (exploding) or experience internally (stuffing).

Self-effort alone can't tame the tongue and our raw emotions that run wild.

Self-effort alone can't tame the tongue and our raw emotions that run wild.

James then goes on to address the exploders whose lack of restraint and brutal honesty result in a very mixed message:

> With the tongue we praise our Lord and Father, and with it
> we curse human beings, who have been made in God's likeness.

Out of the same mouth come praise and cursing. My brothers and sisters, this should not be. Can both fresh water and salt water flow from the same spring? My brothers and sisters, can a fig tree bear olives, or a grapevine bear figs? Neither can a salt spring produce fresh water. (James 3:9 – 12)

Ouch, ouch, ouch. Hold on just a second while I rub my toes that have just been stepped on in a really good way. I love how James doesn't just warn us about what shouldn't be — he goes on to share wisdom about how to recover from times when our exploding honesty hasn't been reined in by godliness.

Who is wise and understanding among you? Let them show it by their good life, by deeds done in the humility that comes from wisdom. (James 3:13)

And there, my friends, is the perfect solution to making our honesty also godly. Our words must be spoken in the humility that comes from wisdom. When we are humble, we realize our honesty can't be one-sided. We make an effort to see the situation from the other person's vantage point. And when we are wise, we pause and measure our words to get at the heart of the issue without sabotaging the heart of our offender.

James also has wisdom for the stuffer:

But if you harbor bitter envy and selfish ambition in your hearts, do not boast about it or deny the truth. Such "wisdom" does not come down from heaven but is earthly, unspiritual, demonic. For where you have envy and selfish ambition, there you find disorder and every evil practice. (James 3:14 – 16)

Oh gracious, time to rub my toes again. And rub the sides of my head too. The harboring that James is referring to here is rooted in envy and selfish ambition. At first glance, I'm not sure this applies to all my stuffing situations. But when I look at the descriptive words *bitter* and *selfish*, that hits the heart of my stuffing every time. I stuff to protect myself by keeping conflict at bay. But if I'm stuffing and not being honest about my true feelings, that self-protection quickly turns into selfishness, and the unresolved conflict gives birth to bitterness. Listen, again, to the wisdom of the apostle James:

> But the wisdom that comes from heaven is first of all pure; then peace-loving, considerate, submissive, full of mercy and good fruit, impartial and sincere. (James 3:17)

I love these qualities! All of them offer wisdom that leads the stuffer to soul integrity, but the last one packs the strongest punch — *sincere*. In other words, our peacemaking efforts must be honest.

Yes, we're after soul integrity — honesty that is godly. This soul integrity brings balance to unglued reactions. It makes us true peacemakers — people who aren't stuffing or exploding but rather honestly demonstrating what they are experiencing in a godly manner. And being a true peacemaker reaps a harvest of great qualities in our lives: right things, godly things, healthy things. Interestingly enough, James wraps up with this exact thought clearly stated: "Peacemakers who sow in peace reap a harvest of righteousness" (James 3:18).

Now I'm the first to admit, dealing with any of these four reactions, intertwined as they are with our personalities and relationships, can be complicated. There aren't quick fixes or easy formulas that guarantee good outcomes when it comes to solving the puzzles of our unglued reactions. But if I can identify the kind of reaction I'm having and I've studied possible healthy solutions, I feel much more empowered to handle my raw emotions with soul integrity.

Maybe right now would be a good time for you to review this chapter and make some notes beside the description of each reaction. Think of the different people in your life and the kinds of reactions you have toward them. Are you like me and you see yourself in all four reactions, or do you relate to only one or two? Don't rush to my suggestions in the next chapters before you've allowed the Lord to show you everything that He wants to show you in this moment. [If you'd like to use a basic self-assessment to help you determine your reaction type(s), see the appendix beginning on page 193.] Once you've done the hard work of inner inspection, you'll be ready to move on and dig a little deeper to unpack more fully all four reactions.

The Exploders

I was standing in the checkout line at Target when the lady behind me tapped me on the shoulder. "Ma'am?" I turned and smiled, wondering if we knew each other. Or thinking maybe she was going to ask in what aisle I'd found the cute necklace I was purchasing. Or maybe I'm making such good imperfect progress with all this unglued stuff she was going to tell me, "You is kind. You is smart. You is important."

Oh I wish.

In an apologetic tone she whispered, "Ma'am, do you know your shirt is on inside out?"

Awesome.

Isn't that so like life? We're just buying a necklace at Target and out of the blue we're hit with, "Your shirt is inside out." My shirt was on inside out because I was so stinkin' distracted by the hurtful conversation I couldn't stop replaying in my head while getting dressed that morning. I had gotten a text message from an exploder and it rattled me. Instead of pausing, I called the sender right away while trying to remain calm. Key word: *trying*. But in the end, I didn't. I was flustered with my emotion that bubbled up. I was flustered by her tone. I was flustered she'd made a big deal out of something that really shouldn't have been a big deal. And obviously all that fluster-ization (great new word) affected even the way I got dressed.

For you, maybe it's not an inside-out shirt in the Target check-out line. Maybe it's a purse that got bumped and flipped upside down. Your wallet, sixty-five old receipts, a half-eaten bagel, pennies, gum, and more pennies spill out along with two tampons and a lip gloss. In the middle of buying something at the church bake sale. Perfect. Of course your mother is there to offer words of comfort that come out something like, "I know I've taught you better than this. Good gosh, why is your purse such a mess? And put on some of that lip gloss while you're down there. You look pale." And the tension mounts. It will take just the slightest thing to twist you beyond what you can bear and you'll fly off the handle. Again.

Or maybe you tell your child no in the grocery store, and she picks that public moment to behave more horridly than she ever has at any other time in her entire life. While discreetly trying to contain the flailing arms, legs, and snot of a screaming child, you stand there on the edge of your own meltdown and wonder, *Where in heavens did this come from? I mean, one minute I'm calmly deciding between grilled chicken or vegetable soup for dinner and the next minute I am the focus of everyone's judgmental glances. All I want to do is throw my purse over my head and scream. Scream! Scream!*

Raw emotions won't sit quietly awaiting further instructions. They'll move — outward if we explode and inward if we stuff.

That's what makes raw emotions so complicated. They come from out of nowhere and run us slap-over. Which is why it's so important to prepare in advance for what will surely happen during your next trip to Target — or while attending the unpredictable family reunion, driving unruly kids in the car pool, or dealing with difficult people at the office. Or when, at the next Bible study meeting, you happen to sit by the woman with the special ministry of discouragement. Or when this month's credit card bill is twice as much as you thought it would be — and there are no fraudulent charges.

In each of these situations and hundreds more we could surely sit around and swap stories about, the raw emotions will come. And when they do, they won't sit quietly awaiting further instructions. They'll move — outward if we explode and inward if we stuff.

As mentioned in the last chapter, I can be an exploder who later shames herself for not acting more patient in the moment. I can also be an exploder who blames others, a stuffer who builds barriers, and a stuffer who collects retaliation rocks.

But that's not where I am staying. And neither are you. So let's "go there" over the course of the next two chapters and see what we can do about it. First up: the exploder who shames herself.

The Exploder Who Shames Herself

That awful, sluggish feeling was begging me to silence the alarm on my phone and roll back over. I wasn't rested enough for another full day. A *very* full day. Still half asleep, I began a mental walk-through of the day's to-do list ... five kids in five different schools. One needs a math tutor. One just broke her braces yesterday and needs an emergency orthodontist appointment. I had to tuck in a conference call while helping my teenage son practice his driving skills.

Oh, heavens! How am I going to participate on a conference call while gasping for air and yelling, "Stop!" every five minutes!? Okay, reschedule the conference call after I pack lunches and shoo everyone out, out, out or we'll be late, late, late. Always late. And if I don't get up right this second we'll be late all over again.

My sluggish feeling had turned into sheer exhaustion and the day hadn't even begun. I picked up my phone to check the time and saw that several emails had arrived overnight.

My soul warned me: *Do not check in with the screaming demands of the world before you exchange whispers with God.* I'd included that little bit of wisdom in a message I'd given to a crowd of people just the weekend before. Part of me wanted to take my own advice, but a bigger part of me didn't.

My curiosity won out, and I clicked open one of the emails as I turned on the bath water to fill the tub and walked into my closet to find something to wear. To protect all involved, I'm changing the details of this story, but my emotional reactions are portrayed exactly as they happened.

The first line of the email was, "Shame on you."

Lovely.

It was from a fellow middle school parent who was deeply offended her daughter hadn't been invited to my daughter's birthday party. Take note of two words in that last sentence that strike fear deep within the hearts of many, many mothers: *middle school.* Need I say more? Glory be.

Never mind that my daughter had been having problems with this girl hurting her feelings all year. Never mind we'd decided to invite only the girls in her homeroom class, of which this girl was not part. And never mind we wished we could invite this girl, but the fear of her repeating the hurt she'd caused in school sent my daughter into a crying fit.

So, we didn't invite her. I'm not saying this was the right decision. But honestly, it wasn't done out of spite at all. We'd done so many things to reach out and extend love to this girl, and my daughter was just completely worn out from continually getting nothing but hurt back. It was a tough decision and one I didn't make lightly.

But, still, I got a shame-on-you email — on the same day I was exhausted and trying to figure out how to get everybody everywhere.

Not only did I get the shame-on-you email, but this other mom was clear about her plans to have my daughter called into the principal's office and reminded to be kind to her daughter.

I don't know what the official definition of a *twit* is. Nor am I completely sure *twit* is a real word. However, when you feel all twisted up, with irritation sprinkled on top, *twit* seems fitting.

So, there I was in a twit right at the start of a new day.

Typically, I am a middle school parent who stays out of the drama. And I readily admit when my kids need to be corrected and redirected. But on this day I could envision myself zinging the person who hurt me with the perfect comeback. This mom had dumped a bucket of hurt on me. The scale tipped heavily on my side. Therefore, I should dump a bucket of hurt on her. Then the scales would be even and my twit would dissipate in this balance of hurt equality. But something in my spirit didn't feel any better after I mentally walked through this leveling of the scales.

I felt heavy.

Here I was, about to be an exploder who would later feel shame for not acting more like someone who really loves Jesus and follows Him. Thankfully, being able to identify my tendency helped me see in advance the downside of the reaction I was about to have. I imagined myself feeling the shame of exploding on this woman, and I didn't like how it felt. I didn't want shame to be my reality.

Sip the shame so you won't have to guzzle the regret.

I'll sometimes say to myself, "Sip the shame so you won't have to guzzle the regret." In other words, taste a little bit of the shame of letting it all rip before you find yourself drowning in gallons of unwanted regret.

Sipping the shame of what would be if I let my raw emotions have their way helped me not explode. And that's good. But I still had some processing to do to make the hurtful feelings dissipate, to deal with my very honest feelings that were not yet very godly.

The last thing we want to do is trade our unhealthy exploding for unhealthy stuffing. Remember, the balance between the two is soul integrity where our honesty is godly. What I needed now was some God perspective.

Finding My Soul Integrity in God's Perspective

Knowing what we need doesn't always translate into wanting what we need. The last thing I wanted in that moment was a Bible verse to come marching my way. I was in a twit. And I don't know about you, but it's hard to pick up the Bible when I feel that way. So I closed my eyes and said, "God, the next time I see her, can I slap her?"

Not that I ever would seriously slap her. I was just in such a bad spot I wanted to envision doing so. Awful, huh? (Again, sip the shame so you won't have to guzzle the regret.)

It took me several hours to pick up my Bible, but when I did, I knew I needed to review the verse in Ephesians 6 that talks about how our enemies are not flesh and blood. And I discovered something new and fresh in this very familiar chapter. But before we get to the new, fresh part, let's review Ephesians 6:12:

> For our struggle is not against flesh and blood, but against the rulers, against the authorities, against the powers of this dark world and against the spiritual forces of evil in the heavenly realms.

I felt like my enemy was the shame-on-you woman, but this passage revealed the truth. In God's economy, people don't stand on opposing sides of the conflict scale. People stand on one side and Satan stands on the other. When we dump hurt into one another's lives, we aren't leveling the conflict scale. We are just weighing down the people side of the scale and elevating the Satan side of the scale. Satan loves it when we do his work for him by dumping on each other.

The secret to healthy conflict resolution isn't taking a you-against-me stance, but realizing it's all of us against Satan—he's the real enemy. But this is hard to do when all we see is that flesh-and-blood person standing there who, quite honestly, is planted squarely on the last good nerve we have left.

Satan loves it when we do his work for him by dumping on each other.

Such a moment may seem like the perfect time to set our Christianity on the shelf. But in fact, it's hands-down one of the grandest opportunities we have to shame Satan back to hell. A Jesus girl who rises up and unexpectedly gives grace when she surely could have done otherwise reveals the power and the mystery of Christ at work —in her life and in the world.

That's why Paul ends Ephesians 6 by making a specific statement about words—how he wants to use them and the impact he wants them to have. This is the fresh, new part. This was the part I hadn't seen and connected with before. After explaining that Satan is our real enemy, reminding us to put on our spiritual armor each day, and reiterating the absolute necessity of prayer, Paul says one more thing:

> Pray also for me, that whenever I open my mouth, words may be given me so that I will fearlessly make known the mystery of the gospel. (Ephesians 6:19 NIV 1984)

The placement of this verse is crucial and intentional. After we remember who the real enemy is—and that the person who hurt us is not our enemy—we must carefully consider the words we speak to this person. After all, it's one thing to make the mental shift that this person isn't my enemy, but quite another to speak words that make known the mystery of the gospel. What a choice!

Still nursing my hurt, I wanted the verse to say, "Most of the time when you open your mouth, make known the gospel. But when someone sends you a shame-on-you email, that day is the exception. Feel free to explode all over her."

Or, "Most of the time when you open your mouth, make known the gospel. But when someone else has obvious issues, you should make her aware of those issues and heap back on her what she's heaped on you."

Or, "Most of the time when you open your mouth, make known the gospel. But if you're feeling really, really hurt, rally other people around your cause and make this other person look as bad as you can."

But that's not what Ephesians 6:19 says. It says I must make the gospel known *whenever* I open my mouth. Is this easy? Of course not! To have any chance at all, I have to develop a strategy in advance for how I will react in situations like these. In advance means I don't wait until I receive the hurtful comment or the shame-on-you email. In a non-emotional, clearheaded moment, I craft a response template. Then, on that day when another person decides to get all up in my Kool-Aid with their own raw emotions, I can hold onto my soul integrity.

Crafting My Response Template

I'm trying to remember not to let my lips or typing fingertips be the first thing that walks into a conflict. My tongue is powerful and holds the potential for death and life. So does sending a piercing text or email response.

That's exactly why I need a response template. I developed this in a very emotionally neutral moment, which is the best time to think through things with the godly honesty of soul integrity. In a heated moment of frustration or anger, I need this preplanned template to keep me from spewing. So, here's what I came up with when I need a written response. Of course this same thought pattern can be tweaked slightly and used for face-to-face interactions as well. Feel free to use what I came up with or come up with your own version to use the next time you need a written or verbal response.

1. Begin by honoring the one offended.

This isn't easy. We probably won't feel like the other person deserves honor in that moment. And maybe they don't. I certainly didn't feel like honoring my offender's words. So, I didn't honor her words. I honored her as a person — a person God loves. I have to remember that giving honor reveals more about my character than the character of the other person.

Here's how I did this... *Dear Sally, I can tell you are a mother who cares deeply for your child.*

I honored her by pointing out a good quality I know to be true about her. Even if you have to think really hard about what good qualities your offender has, most everyone does have redeeming qualities.

2. Keep your response short and full of grace.

The wordier we get, the greater the risk we will slip into defensiveness. If something needs to be clarified, keep it concise and wrapped in grace.

Here are the lines I wrote:

A line to acknowledge the expressed hurt: *I understand how hard it can be when we feel our child has been left out. Like you, I hurt when my child hurts.*

A line to clarify my intentions: *Might I share from my heart what I intended when we invited only the girls from Hope's homeroom class? Hope would have invited many more if she could. But this seemed the fairest way to keep the party manageable.*

A line of gentle honesty about the issue at hand: *This has been a hard year on Hope. You are probably aware of the conflicts Hope and your daughter have had. If you'd like to discuss some possible ways we can better guide both girls in their actions and reactions toward one another, I would welcome that.*

And, if an apology is appropriate: *Please accept my most sincere apology for causing you and your daughter hurt.*

A line asking for grace: *Thank you for extending me grace in this situation.*

3. End by extending compassion.

Chances are this person is hurting for reasons that have nothing to do with this situation. We'll discuss this at length in another chapter. For now, why not be the rare person who offers love to this hard-to-love person ... *With more love and compassion than these words can hold, Lysa.*

Of course, if it's not possible to sincerely end your note that way, don't fake it. I know some conflicts can make it impossible to wrap everything with love. So maybe your compassionate close might be a simple: *Blessings ... Thank you ...* or *With grace.*

Please remember, not every harsh email needs a response. I knew mine did. Ask God to help you know when to deal with it and when to simply delete it.

Also, remember not every face-to-face confrontation needs a verbal response either. But when it does, you can easily translate what I've suggested here for the needed conversation. Just keep these three points in mind: Honor them. Keep it short and wrapped with grace. Extend some kind of compassion. Honor, grace, compassion ... H.G.C.

Choosing a gentle reply doesn't mean you're weak. Whether we're face-to-face or sending a written response, we do need to remember there is a big difference between a *reaction* and a *reply*. Reactions are typically harsh words used to prove how wrong the other person is. No good ever comes from this. A gentle reply, on the other hand, "turns away wrath" (Proverbs 15:1). Choosing a gentle reply doesn't mean you're weak; it actually means you possess a rare and godly strength.

I think I'm going to repeat that last sentence, not so much for you but because, glory be, I need it! *Choosing a gentle reply doesn't mean you're weak; it actually means you possess a rare and godly strength.*

So, how did this middle school drama turn out? I sent my reply and didn't hear back from the other mother right away. Eventually, we did wind up having a talk with the girls to help them process the hurt between them and get to a more neutral place. Hope and the other girl never became close friends. They were very different children with different needs in friendship. And that's okay.

I had to keep things in perspective, like the fact that middle school is wonky no matter what and that this too shall pass. I heard something on the radio the other day that gave me a great image of what it means to keep things in perspective. The radio announcer was talking about how freaked out people get when their cats climb up trees. His guest was a firefighter who gets a least one call a week from someone wanting help to get their cat down. The firefighter said, if he has time, he'll help them out, but if he's not able to go, he gently reminds the cat owner that he's never seen a cat skeleton in a tree.

Hmmm. Interesting point. It helped me remember that my child won't be in middle school forever. This other mother who is dealing with her own child's middle school issues won't be in that hard place forever. This all shall pass. And, in the end, it's good for me to remember that it isn't my job to fix this woman with my reply. That's God's job. My job is to be obedient to God in the midst of my own set of issues.

I can't say developing a response template will forever keep us from exploding and then feeling the weight of the after-shame, but it does help us take a more positive step than we would have taken before this journey.

For now, focus on the progress you're making. Thank God for it and pave your journey with grace. Grace for yourself when you're an exploder who shames herself, and grace for yourself when you experience the other side of this coin as an exploder who blames others.

The Exploder Who Blames Others

Every now and then I attempt to be "that mom." You know, the one who wields a glue gun whilst craftifying something worthy of a showcase display at the Hobby Lobby. And the one who joyfully reads aloud to her children without being sneaky and skipping pages. Yes, her.

But it never works out for me.

Take, for example, the brilliant time I decided to attend a book warehouse clearance sale. I loaded up my kids and decided this was the perfect time to help my people fall in love with books. I wrongly figured a sale could help anyone feel the literary love. Not so.

My kids couldn't have cared less about the books.

What they wanted was in a crate off to the side of all the bookshelves. The brightly colored packages were laced with promises. I plucked one from my kid's hands that claimed to contain the coolest-ever science experiment. Anytime a brightly colored package uses the words *cool* and *experiment* on the front, a mother should beware. Especially when said package is marked down to one dollar. She should be very wise and tell her children, "No."

But, tired from all the efforts to convince them to love books, I rationalized that since we'd dedicated our morning to this sale, we should at least walk out with something educational. So, I bought several of the kits.

Sea monkeys. That's what the kits were supposed to grow. Key words: *supposed to*. My kids were beyond excited to get this party started. Into the container went the chemicals, the water, the little food crystals, and plastic green trees upon which the sea monkeys could play once they hatched.

It's at this point I should share that this is one of those good news/bad news stories. Yes ma'am, which would you like first?

The good news ... something did hatch.

The bad news ... it wasn't sea monkeys.

After leaving the experiment overnight, I woke to find my kitchen invaded by the biggest, nastiest, hairiest, giant flies you have ever seen. I'm not sure if our sea monkeys had a mutation situation going on or if some sort of larvae had gotten into the packages and eaten our sea monkeys.

Either way, it was awful.

The moral of this story is simple. Some moms are equipped by the hand of God to be "that mom." They have been formed with the three-C gene — Cooking, Crafting, and Cleaning come easily and naturally to them.

Others of us have been delightfully chosen to provide the comic relief necessary to keep this world entertained. And to keep future therapists in business.

I know this story sounds funny now, but at the time it was yet one more thing that excluded me from belonging to the good mom club. My internal good mom/bad mom dialogue tormented me:

Good moms grow sea monkeys. Bad moms grow nasty flies.

Wait! Good moms don't even buy sea monkey kits at a book sale. Bad moms struggle to tell their kids no and give in too easily.

Good moms get on the Internet and figure out how to turn a fly debacle into an enriching science lesson for their kids. Bad moms kill the stupid flies and hide all evidence from their kids.

On and on the dialogue went. And with each reassurance that I was a bad mom, my emotions ratcheted higher and higher. On a stress scale from 1 to 10, I could have been hovering around 4, but this conversation in my head easily pushed me to 7. Add to that a kid squabble over who licked whose toast at breakfast and the fact that I couldn't find my cell phone, and I was all the way up to 9.8, ready to explode and blame anyone and everyone who had the misfortune to be nearby. What I felt was anger. What I needed was self-control.

I'm trying to understand better this whole concept of self-control. The Bible includes many verses about the subject, among them Proverbs 25:28, Galatians 5:23, and 1 Peter 5:8. But it's hard to display self-control when someone else does things out of my control that yank my emotions into a bad place. So, here's one little tidbit I'm learning. When someone else's actions or statements threaten to pull me into a bad place, I have a choice. I do. It may not feel like it. In fact, it may feel like I am a slave to my feelings —but I'm not. Remember, feelings are indicators, not dictators. They can indicate there is a situation I need to deal with, but they shouldn't dictate how I react. I have a choice.

Feelings are indicators, not dictators.

Self-Control

"I have a choice!" I will sometimes say this out loud in the midst of the angry moment to hold me back from exploding. My choice is whether or not to give the other person the power to control my emotions. The one who holds their tongue is the one who holds the power. When I react by yelling, flying off the handle, or making a snappy comment, I basically transfer my power to the other person. In the case of my children, that means I am giving my power to one of my five teenagers. Yikes.

When I consider my response from this perspective, I quickly realize I don't want to freely hand over my power to someone not in a position to handle it. And I don't want to be placed in a situation where I'm tempted to be more immature than my kids — or anyone else. When I am void of power, I am void of self-control. So, it seems to me, if I'm going to remain self-controlled, I have to keep my power.

Now, when I say "my power," I don't mean something I conjure up myself. I am referring to God's power working in me. When I react according to God's Word, I feel that power. When I react contrary to God's Word, I feel powerless.

God's words in Isaiah offer a good reminder of how we can tap into His power no matter our situation:

> As the rain and the snow come down from heaven, and do not return to it without watering the earth and making it bud and flourish, so that it yields seed for the sower and bread for the eater, so is my word that goes out from my mouth: It will not return to me empty, but will accomplish what I desire and achieve the purpose for which I sent it. (Isaiah 55:10–11)

Did you catch that? God's Word will not return empty! The answer to keeping God's power with me and working in me to produce self-control is letting God's Word get inside me. His Word seeping into my mind and my heart will accomplish things — good things, powerful things, things that help me display self-control. That's how I access God's power.

So, all that to say, here's my new tactic: When I'm facing a situation in which someone is getting on my last good nerve, I'm going to start quoting God's Word in the present tense, either in my head or out loud, depending on the situation. For example, if one of my sweet children starts acting *not so sweet* I might call to mind 1 Peter 5:6–8 and say (or at least think before responding): "In this moment I'm choosing to be self-controlled and alert. Your actions are begging me to yell and lose control. But I realize I have an enemy, and that enemy is not you. The devil is prowling and roaring and looking to devour me through my own lack of control right now, but I am God's girl. That's right, I am. I am going to humbly and quietly let God have His way in me. And when I do, God will lift up me and my frayed nerves from this situation and fill me with a much better reaction than what I can give you at the moment. Give me just a few minutes and then we'll talk calmly about this."

Of course if I were with a coworker or friend, I might excuse myself or ask to call back before talking about the issue. Then I would mentally quote Scripture until my inner being had calmed. Either way, processing things scripturally in the present tense keeps my heart in a much better place.

Now, if I were reading this advice twenty years ago I would have rolled my eyes and thought to myself, *Well isn't that special, she's memorized so much Scripture. But what about a girl like me who barely knows John 3:16?* This isn't an exercise in memorization as much as it is in application. In other words, keep verses handy to use. The ones we've been covering in this book would work well. Record a few that really strike a chord with you in the notes app on your phone, on three-by-five cards, or on sticky notes on your desk. And here's the cool thing: The more you use them, the more likely you'll be to memorize them! This is so important because when we operate according to God's Word, we operate according to God's will.

Girl, that's some power right there. And it will make you shine in so much self-control that your kids, friends, spouse, and coworkers won't know what to do with you.

I'll be honest. Even though I know and teach this principle, there are times I feel that Bible verses on three-by-five cards spoken in the present tense are no match for my explosions.

I get it. But God is the perfect match. Divine communication with Him is what's needed, and sometimes the quickest way for me to receive it is by going straight to His Word. Why divine communication? Because we need God to help us hold back the explosions. Hold back the blaming. And hold back the shaming. Proverbs 29:18 — "Where there is no revelation, people cast off restraint" — is such a good reminder that only revelation or the truth of God's Word can help restrain us the right way. The Hebrew word for "revelation" in this verse is *chazown* (kha-zone), which means divine communication. In other words, "Without *divine communication* people cast off restraint." Interesting, huh?

Holy Restraint

Quoting God's Word in the present tense infuses our hearts with holy restraint and diffuses our reactions so we don't spew. Is this just another form of self-control? No, there's a difference between self-control and holy restraint. Self-control is a fruit of the Holy Spirit. It's the external expression of our relationship with God. Holy restraint is the seed of this fruit. It's the internal experience of living with Christ and really applying His truths to my life. It's deciding I'm not just going to *ingest* His truths by taking them in and feeling good about them for a few minutes. I'm going to *digest* His truths by making them part of who I am and how I live. There's a big difference between ingesting truth and digesting it.

I learned what this all looks like the night my youngest daughter, Brooke, came to me and asked if she could bake a cake—at nine o'clock. After my kitchen was cleaned and closed for the night. Ugh. Nothing in me wanted this child to make a cake. But I'd been to some parenting seminar that encouraged parents not to always instantly say no to their kids. (Why do I go to these seminars?)

Anyhow, Hope, Brooke's older sister, offered to help, and I was too tired to argue with the incessant pleas of a nine-year-old. Brooke measured and poured, whipped and stirred, and carefully placed a batter-filled cake pan into the oven. Then she turned on the oven light and watched the cake bake. Her cake became her whole focus. She couldn't stop looking at the cake and grew increasingly impatient with the slow-passing minutes on the timer.

About thirty minutes into the forty-five-minute baking time, the cake looked done. It smelled done. Brooke wanted it to be done. She reasoned it must be done! Hope helped retrieve the cake and placed it on the counter to cool. For a few minutes it looked fabulous. But it wasn't long until the cake imploded. The cake couldn't withstand the pressure of an undone center ... and neither can we.

We must spend time with God, letting His truths become part of who we are and how we live. That's what it means to have an internal experience with Him. Only then will we develop holy restraint. This holy restraint will hold us back when we want to aggressively charge ahead. It will help us hold our tongues when we want to cut loose instantly with the yelling. It will help us pause before blasting someone in an emotional tirade.

Once we develop that holy restraint from an internal experience with God, we can have external expressions that honor God.

Holy restraint is the seed that produces the fruit of self-control.

Remember, holy restraint is the seed that produces the fruit of self-control. This self-control is the external expression — the evidence — of a well-done center that helps us to respond in more godly ways.

So, yes, God's Word — His divine communication at work in us internally — really can help us externally when we're tempted to be exploders who blame.

Finding the Quiet

Remember, our goal — whether we are exploding and shaming ourselves or exploding and blaming others — is imperfect progress. When I've had an explosion, I feel a lot more *imperfect* than I do *progress*. We're dealing with emotions and relationships ... both of which are like nailing Jell-O to the wall. It's a complicated, messy, and unpredictable process, for sure. Sometimes a girl can get worn out, wonder if she's ever going to stop exploding, and feel like giving up. But before I give up, I've learned to hush up. This often means hitting some sort of pause button on whatever situation is making me feel like exploding. Ideally, this would mean getting away by myself in the quiet of my home. But sometimes it means excusing myself to the restroom. Bathroom stalls can make great prayer closets (smiles). The point is that the only way I can see what God is doing and attend to what He reveals is to get quiet with Him.

Bathroom stalls can make great prayer closets.

Of course, it's hard to be quiet when I'm in a potentially exploding frame of mind. But as we wrap up this chapter, I want to leave you with five beautiful things I've discovered in the quiet, five things that are balm for the raw edges of a soul on the precipice of exploding.

1. In the quiet, we feel safe enough to humble ourselves.

The last thing I want to do in the heat of an emotional mess is to be humble. I want to be loud, proud, and prove my point. But I've learned the hard way that I have to step out of the battle and humbly ask God to speak truth to my heart in order for things to start making sense. Never have I had a relationship issue in which I didn't contribute at least something to the problem. Usually, I can only see this something in the quiet. The quiet is what enables us to "humble [ourselves], therefore, under God's mighty hand" (1 Peter 5:6).

2. In the quiet, God lifts us up to a more rational place.

When we are in the heat of a tangled mess, crazy emotions drag us down into a pit of hopelessness. The only way out of the pit is to make the choice to stop digging deeper and turn to God for a solution, so "that [God] may lift you up in due time" (1 Peter 5:6).

3. In the quiet, anxiety gives way to progress.

We can pour out our anxious hearts to Jesus who loves us right where we are, just as we are. Because His love comes without unfair human judgment, we soften and feel safe enough to humbly admit we need Him to work on us. Trying to fix another person only adds to my anxiety. Letting Jesus work on me is where real progress happens. I claim the promise that says, "Cast all your anxiety on him because he cares for you" (1 Peter 5:7).

4. In the quiet, we acknowledge that our real enemy isn't the other person.

As noted earlier in the chapter, the person with whom we're in conflict may seem like the enemy and might even look like the enemy. But the truth is, that person isn't the real culprit. The real culprit is Satan, who is exerting influence on both me and on the person offending me. I don't always realize this in the heat of the moment, but in the quiet, I can remind myself of the truth and choose a strategy for responding with self-control. That's the wisdom of Scripture, which says, "Be self-controlled and alert. Your enemy the devil prowls around like a roaring lion looking for someone to devour. Resist him, standing firm in the faith" (1 Peter 5:8–9 NIV 1984).

5. In the quiet, I can rest assured God will use this conflict for good—no matter how it turns out.

If I make the effort to handle this conflict well, I can be freed from the pressure to make everything turn out rosy. Sometimes relationships grow stronger through conflict; other times relationships end. Because I can't control the other person, I must focus on the good God is working out in me through this situation and leave the outcome with Him. God's Word promises that "the God of all grace, who called you to his eternal glory in Christ, after you have suffered a little while, will himself restore you and make you strong, firm, and steadfast" (1 Peter 5:10).

Add to this list as you discover your own benefits for intentionally getting quiet when all you really want to do is explode.

Oh God, help us — help me. I want to be a passionate woman reined in by You and Your grace . . . not an exploder who shames herself or blames others. I want to sip the shame so I won't have to guzzle the regret. I want to be the one who holds her tongue and keeps the Holy Spirit's power working in me. I want these truths to sink in and become part of who I am and how I live.

And I know that's what You want too.

Imperfect progress.

Can you sense you're headed toward this goal?

The Stuffers

I'm an encourager at heart. I love to give words of encouragement and I love to receive words of encouragement. That's probably why words of *dis*couragement affect me so deeply. I don't mind constructive criticism given in a spirit of love. But when someone hasn't taken the time to invest words of encouragement in my life before offering some sort of constructive criticism, it doesn't feel so constructive. You know what I mean?

When I was a young mom I had a friend who was much more scheduled and plan oriented with her mothering than me. Her kids took naps at the exact same time every day. She didn't give her kids sugar. And they got a bath, complete with a hair washing, every night before bed.

I admired her. But I wasn't like her. My kids often took their naps in the car between errands. I always had a little baggie of M&M's in my purse—just in case. As for baths, my kids were always clean but, heavens, it never seemed necessary to wash their hair every day.

I just did the best I could.

But my "best" bothered this very put-together friend. And she wasn't shy about sharing her disapproval with me. I always knew a criticism was coming when she'd start a sentence with, "Wow, I can't believe you let your kids …" Or, "Aren't you worried how _____ is going to affect your kids long-term?" Or, "Hmmm, my husband and I don't believe in …"

I would find myself swallowing the hurt in bitter gulps. But never once did I tell her how much her criticisms affected me. I just took it. And took it. And took it. Until one day I couldn't take it anymore. I stopped going to the Bible study we attended together, made excuses about being busy when she called me, and put so much distance between us the relationship went away completely.

I regret this now.

Despite her being very vocal about her parenting style preferences, she really was a good friend. And I think we could have learned a lot from one another. Maybe I could have helped her relax a tad and maybe she could have helped me be a bit more intentional. I'll never know because I chose to stuff the hurt and sever the relationship.

As I examined my own propensities to stuff and read thousands of comments on my blog, I discovered two types of stuffer reactions: stuffers who build barriers and stuffers who collect retaliation rocks. There are several reasons I find myself stuffing.

I stuff because:

- I don't feel safe enough to confront this person.
- I don't have the energy or the time to get into a conflict right now.
- I don't know how to address the issue.
- I don't want to seem hypersensitive.
- I don't want to get rejected.
- I don't want to lose control.
- I don't want to make things worse, so I convince myself I can just let it go.

But if I'm completely honest, as a Christian woman I also sometimes stuff because it feels more godly. Verses like Proverbs 10:19 prompt: "Too much talk leads to sin. Be sensible and keep your mouth shut" (NLT). And I plant in my brain, "It's godly to hold back my words." Then I reinforce my thinking with a verse like Proverbs 15:18: "A hot-tempered person stirs up conflict, but the one who is patient calms a quarrel."

As a Christian woman I sometimes stuff because it feels more godly.

I want to keep the peace. I want to be gentle, not confrontational. And these are good things—if I can do them without harboring bitterness. That's called healthy processing. But there's a big difference between healthy processing and stuffing.

I engage in healthy processing when I work through the issue and diffuse the hurt. Maybe I do this through prayer and studying my Bible. Maybe I do it by talking to a counselor or mentor in my life. Maybe I give it enough time that I come to realize it's not such a big deal after all. But here's the key: The end result is that the hard feelings dissipate. If they don't, they get stuffed. And that's the trouble.

As noted in chapter 4, the two ways stuffers react are either to build barriers or to collect retaliation rocks. And neither of these reactions leads to conflict restoration, but instead to relational decimation and conflict escalation. And, at the risk of sounding like a totally cheesy poet, that's no underestimation.

The Stuffer Who Builds Barriers

Have you ever tried to keep the peace by avoiding confrontation and pretending that everything is fine? I have. I just stuff down the negative emotions. And it hurts. It hurts me. It hurts the other person. And it certainly hurts the relationship, which slowly erodes.

What seems like peace on the outside is actually the muffled roar of barrier-building activity on the inside.

Barriers shut down communication. When you determine that other people aren't safe, you label them with words such as *demanding, irresponsible, volatile, selfish*, and *defensive*. No matter what they do or don't do, this barrier label is the filter through which you process everything about them. Mentally, you just stick it across a person's name in your brain. The problem is: They don't know it's there. So every interaction confuses them. They know something is wrong but have no clue what it is. Eventually, this relationship will shrivel up and die because it's been deprived of open communication, the life-giving oxygen that fuels good relationships.

Open communication is the life-giving oxygen that fuels good relationships.

Barriers or Boundaries?

What we need is boundaries, not barriers. Boundaries are simply clearly stated parameters that provide a safe structure for communication and the health of a relationship. It may be difficult for some people to accept the boundaries we set, but at least the boundaries offer clarity rather than confusion about the status of the relationship. Here are some examples of clearly communicated, healthy boundaries:

- "If you continue being thirty minutes late to events, I will take a separate car."
- "I need a better work ethic from you in the office, or we'll have to make some changes."
- "If you keep spending over our budget, I will cut up the credit cards."
- "I can't lend you any more money until I see you making serious efforts to find a job."

- "I want to bring your grandkids to see you, but if you just surf the Web while we're there, it's not worth it to come."

- "If you won't stop drinking too much or using drugs, I will take the kids and move out."[4]

The difference between boundaries and barriers is honest transparency. When we erect a barrier with a person, it's either because we're afraid to be honest, tired of being honest and getting hurt, or feel like the relationship isn't worth the hard work honesty sometimes takes.

The difference between boundaries and barriers is honest transparency.

When we establish boundaries, we are brave enough to be honest but also compassionate enough to wrap the boundary in grace by clearly communicating the parameters of the relationship. Barriers set relationships on a regressive course that leads to isolation. Boundaries set relationships on a progressive course that leads to connection.

The destructive isolation that happens with stuffers who build barriers doesn't limit itself to just one relationship in that person's life. It becomes an entrenched pattern that impacts many relationships, which is why it's so crucial to break the pattern. "Whoever isolates himself seeks his own desire; he breaks out against all sound judgment" (Proverbs 18:1 ESV). *The Message* version of this verse says, "Loners who care only for themselves spit on the common good." Wow.

Yes, we must break this pattern, but how?

What Do I Really Want?

I know I need to learn how to gracefully express honest transparency. But sometimes I give in to fear instead and find myself dancing around an issue rather than facing it head-on. The more I dance around, the more emotional yuck gets pulled into the situation. It's exhausting. And frustrating.

Obviously, I've been around this bush a time or two hundred.

The most important thing I've learned I must do to communicate with graceful honesty and transparency is to identify what I really want. Don't read over that last part too quickly. Think about it. I have to ask myself, *What do I really want in this situation?* Then I have to determine how realistic or unrealistic that want is. If it's unrealistic, I may have to process it with the other person until we can agree on a solution that *is* realistic.

Here's an example of how this played out for me recently. I had a meeting with my staff at the Proverbs 31 office. I don't often go into the office because with all my weekend traveling for speaking engagements, it's better for me to work from home during the week.

Anyhow, I walked in and saw that my staff had turned my office into a much needed storage room and distributed my office furniture to other people who could make use of it every day. We had previously talked about doing this and I had agreed it was a wise decision, but something about seeing it done so quickly caught me off guard and ignited conflicting feelings in my heart.

The rational part of my brain affirmed that this was good; the emotional part of my heart struggled. When I went home that day, I had a choice to make. I could get all caught up in the emotion and make this a much bigger deal than it needed to be, or I could sit with Jesus and ask for a better perspective.

I've often chosen the emotional route. And honey, let me tell you, that's an exhausting road for sure. As a card-carrying member of the stuff-it-and-smile-on-the-outside-while-you-scream-on-the-inside club, it's a road I've traveled and will no doubt travel again. It's part of my DNA — and my PMS. But on this occasion, some rare rationality tugged me into just sitting with Jesus and seeking wisdom.

As I sat, I sensed the Lord whispering, "What do you really want?"

"I want to pout, wallow in how justified my pouting is, and pout some more," I prayed in response. "And then I want to swallow this bitterness and act a little distant from these girls for a while."

But that wasn't really true. It was how I *felt*, but it wasn't what I *wanted*. There is a big difference between the two. And, in the end, it was identifying the difference between what I felt and what I wanted that led to a good solution — which is always the goal when tackling conflict.

I knew that my feelings should be indicators, not dictators. My feelings about the office indicated I needed to process some emotions so my feelings wouldn't dictate my response. And when I considered what was most important to me, I realized what I really wanted was an office at home. A real office. Not a kitchen table with piles of stuff here and there, but an organized space to call my own.

Naming what I really wanted helped me cut through the emotion and focus on a good solution. I called my office manager and told her I was thinking of setting up a home office. She was incredibly supportive and told me that, when I was ready, I could either have my furniture from the Proverbs 31 office or the ministry would help me purchase some new furniture. (By the way, I finally did set up a home office and have posted pictures on *pinterest@lysaterkeurst* if you want to see.)

No tangled feelings. No big issue. No stuffing and labeling my office gals as uncaring — which is a good thing because they are the most caring, loving, heartwarming people you'll ever meet. How tragic it would have been for me to stuff and build a barrier that could have been blown way out of proportion and undermined my relationships with people I care so much about.

Now, I realize this is a small situation compared to many others we'll face. But there's something to this process of thinking past the emotion and identifying what we really want. At least if we know what we're after, we can be equipped to express our concerns with honesty, transparency, and grace.

Of course, the gals at my office made this a much smoother processing situation because of their kind and responsive grace back to me. But what about seemingly impossible situations with seemingly impossible people?

Impossible People

Before we move on to the stuffer who collects retaliation rocks, I want to address the issue of impossible people. We know that all things are possible with God. But all things are not possible with people who refuse to be led by the Holy Spirit.

I've had to get really honest about certain people in my life. It isn't productive or possible to confront them and expect anything good to come from it. If someone has told me over and over through their actions and reactions that they will make my life miserable if I confront them, at some point I have to back away.

But I don't want to stuff and allow bitterness toward them to poison me. So, how do I back away and not stuff?

I acknowledge that I can control only myself. I can't control how another person acts or reacts. Therefore, I shift my focus from trying to fix the other person and the situation to allowing God to reveal some tender truths to me. I typically pray something like this: *God, I'm so tired of being hurt. I'm so tired of feeling distracted and discouraged by this situation. Pour Your lavish mercy on my heart and into this hard relationship. Help me to see the obvious hurt they must have in their life that makes them act this way. Help me to have compassion for their pain. Help me to see anything I'm doing or have done that has negatively affected this situation. And please help me to know how to separate myself graciously from this constant source of hurt in my life. It all feels*

My job isn't to fix the difficult people in my life or enable them to continue disrespectful or abusive behaviors.

impossible. Oh God, speak to me. Reveal clearly how I can best honor You, even in this.

My job isn't to fix the difficult people in my life or enable them to continue disrespectful or abusive behaviors. My job is to be obedient to God in the way I act and respond to those people. Here's how my friend, Pastor Craig Groeschel, describes what it means to back away from a difficult person:

> If you try faithfully to establish healthy boundaries with a toxic person and the person continues to abuse, criticize, threaten, tempt, or harm you, it's time to cut off the toxic relationship. The right thing to do is sever the relationship to protect yourself.
>
> To be crystal clear, I'm not talking about divorcing your spouse. We don't divorce, abandon, or cut off our spouses just because we are having a difficult time. If you are having a tough time in your marriage, don't run into the bedroom shouting, "You're toxic so I'm leaving you!" Instead, call your pastor or a Christian counselor and work on your marriage. Let me say it again, I'm not talking about divorce here.
>
> I'm also not talking about cutting off one of your family members. It must break God's heart how often a parent writes off a child or a sibling stops speaking to another. With the exception of extreme abuse, most problems can be resolved. But every now and then, if a relationship is so toxic that it threatens the spiritual health (or physical safety) of another, then it's time to amputate.
>
> We see several examples of cutting off relationships in the Bible. When Paul and Barnabas had a sharp disagreement, rather than fighting about it, going to court, or gossiping all over town, they decided to go their separate ways (see Acts 15).[5]

When I read those words by Pastor Craig, something in my heart settled. I realized that neither Paul nor Barnabas were bad people.

They were good people. But they weren't good together. And that's okay. It's so much healthier to be brave enough to go your separate ways than to keep stuffing and drown in a sea of bitterness.

We are instructed by the apostle Paul, "Do not repay anyone evil for evil. Be careful to do what is right in the eyes of everyone. If it is possible, as far as it depends on you, live at peace with everyone" (Romans 12:17–18). I pay special attention to the "as far as it depends on you" part. I can't control another person, but I *can* control whether or not I repay evil for evil. I *can* be careful with my actions. I *can* do what is right. But only as far as it depends on me —in other words, I can only make this progress on behalf of myself. I can't compel other people into this kind of progress if they aren't willing to pursue peace with me.

If they make the choice to walk over me rather than walk with me, I'll have to love them from afar. I can forgive and refuse to hold resentment toward them, but just because I extend my forgiveness doesn't mean I have to give them access to me.

Of course, all of this must be handled with much prayer because every situation and every relationship is uniquely complex. But I can't ignore the obvious issues and hope things will somehow miraculously get better on their own. *I* have to get better. I have to take the necessary steps to keep my soul integrity intact. I have to pursue being the person God wants me to be regardless of how other people react.

Yes, I want the soul integrity that comes from healthy boundaries in my life. And I now know whether I continue in relationship with a person or not, it's never healthy to build a barrier and keep stuffing. But what about those times you stuff down only to have an eventual explosion of all you've pushed within? That's the second kind of stuffer: the one who collects retaliation rocks.

The Stuffer Who Collects Retaliation Rocks

As I write, the news is full of stories about the tenth anniversary of the 9/11 terrorist attacks. Because of the catastrophic events that took place on this day, most of us remember where we were and what we were doing when we first heard about the horrors at the World Trade Center, the Pentagon, and in a field southeast of Pittsburgh. I remember. But it pains me to do so.

I was standing in my kitchen staring down at the phone, mentally reciting all the reasons my fury was justified. Art had made me so mad that morning. It was just another little thing added on top of too many other stuffed things, and the accumulated impact had pushed me into the retaliation zone. When Art called me on his way to work, all the stuffing I'd been doing for months blasted out in a long list of everything I felt was wrong with him. When he didn't respond to my tirade the way I wanted him to, I slammed down the phone.

Then I stared. And fumed. And made hateful lists.

Art called back a few minutes later. "What do you want!?" I said, every word dripping with bitterness.

His voice was surprisingly somber. "Lys, turn on the TV. I think you should go get the kids from school." I picked up the television remote and clicked. I gasped. And when I saw the second plane hit the World Trade Center, I immediately jumped into my car to pick up my children from school.

In the weeks that followed, I watched hundreds of stories unfold on the news. And I intentionally faced up to the cold, hard reality that I had taken love for granted. So very for granted.

I don't enjoy remembering the awful fight Art and I had on that frightful day, but I do try to remember the clearheadedness it gave me about what's really important to me. Many people sent their loved ones off to work or the airport that day and never saw them again. What if my stuffed-then-spewed words had been the last conversation I'd ever had with my husband? That thought made me shudder. And I don't say that in a cheesy, feel-the-emotion-in-the-moment kind of way. I say it in a perspective-changing way. A way that shook me and made me realize how damaging stuffing and collecting retaliation rocks can be.

I love my husband and I love keeping the peace between us. But I feel so safe with my husband that I'll act out in ways with him I wouldn't dare act out with others. With others I am cool, calm, and collected. With the man I love I can get quiet in a mean way. That means my outside is quiet, but my inside is anything but. Beneath the surface, I am an emotional stone factory, churning out rocks—rocks I'll collect and collect and collect and collect. Until one day, wham! Something happens and all that stuffing erupts, and I rock his world—literally.

I stuff as a false way to keep the peace. True peacekeeping isn't about stopping the emotion. Remember, emotions move—inward or outward—whether we want them to or not. True peacekeeping is about properly processing the emotions before they get stuffed and rot into something horribly toxic.

Processing Questions

So, how do we process these emotions before stuffing them? As I mentioned before, perspective helps. My friend Holly always asks herself, *If I knew this person wasn't coming home tonight, would I still let this bother me?* That's a good quick question to ask to keep the little things from turning into bigger things.

Another good question is, *Will I still remember what I'm so mad about a month from now?* If the answer is no, I should probably process the situation and let it go. Honestly, I can't remember what made me so mad on 9/11. But I sure do remember my unreasonably escalated and inappropriate response. Yes, perspective helps.

But what about bigger things—lingering hurts, ongoing issues, situations that keep repeating themselves—that we can't seem to let go of as easily? We need a strategy to process those as well. If we don't deal with the bigger things heaped on our rock pile, we'll be especially vulnerable to an explosion of rock-throwing retaliation later. In the next chapter, we'll talk more about developing a personal plan for handling conflicts. But for now, allow me to describe the strategy I use to deal with rocks I'm stuffing.

I ask myself one crucial question—so crucial, might I dare say, that *not* asking it will lead to conflict escalation rather than relationship restoration. So, what is this crucial question?

Am I trying to *prove* or *improve*?

In other words, is my desire in this conflict to *prove that I am right*, or is my desire to *improve the relationship*?

Am I trying to prove that I am right or to improve the relationship?

When I try to prove I am right, I use the stuffed emotion to justify my rock manufacturing activity. Hurt upon hurt builds rock upon rock as I amass lots of proof that I am right and the other person is wrong. Then, when my stuffing eventually leads to an explosion, I am armed with a rock pile of past hurts and offenses and ready to make my case. Prove my case. Win my case, at all costs. I react from a place of hurt and anger and say things I later regret.

On the other hand, when my desire is to improve the relationship, I seek to understand where the other person is coming from and care enough about the relationship to fight for it rather than against it. Instead of reacting out of anger, I pause and let the Holy Spirit redirect my first impulses.

Then I tackle the *issues*, not the *person*.

When I tackle an issue, I ask more questions. I know it may seem like I ask myself lots of questions, but that's how I process. And while sometimes that processing is internal, there are also times when external processing with the other person is good and necessary. External processing is a great diffuser because it forces me to channel all that pent-up frustration in a proactive way and thus handle the situation rather than harm the relationship.

Consider these questions that have helped me to redirect my focus from proving myself to improving the relationship:

- Will you help me understand why you feel this way?
- Can we both agree to stick to the issue at hand and not pull in past issues?
- What is a good desired outcome in this situation?
- How can we meet in the middle on this issue?
- What is something good that can come out of this issue — something that will improve our relationship moving forward?

Of course, one must ask the questions with the right tone and an honest desire to better understand the other person. (Trust me, I've asked with a snarky attitude and seriously impeded any progress!) But said in the right tone, it's so much better to throw out a gentle question than a bitter, condemning rock.

Art and I have renamed what we used to call fights. We now call our occasional spats "growth opportunities." And isn't growth a desirable goal in any relationship? Working on healthy strategies is worth it. Even if we do it all imperfectly, any progress is good. After all, we are the ones who benefit from healthy processing. Our relationships will improve. Our outlooks will be more positive. We'll start to see biblical truths come alive in our lives, which will strengthen our relationships with God. And we'll learn to identify rough edges within ourselves that need attention ... such as unrealistic expectations.

Dealing with Unrealistic Expectations

Unrealistic expectations are often the seeds of bitterly stuffed emotions. I've had to get very honest with myself about my own expectations. Sometimes, when my reality doesn't measure up to my ideal, I'm left feeling slighted.

Have you ever done this with a relationship?

You wish your husband would be more romantic, so you develop expectations for him to rise up suddenly with a bouquet of flowers and poetic words that make you swoon. You hope he'll stay off the phone when the two of you are together. You'd love it if he'd be more involved with the kids when he gets home from work and help you clean the kitchen after dinner. Or maybe you just wish he'd hold you.

You wish your mom were more like your friend's mom, who is actively engaged and helpful with the children. So you develop expectations for her to suddenly be super-grandma, wielding a crafting kit and a burning desire to help you. You long for her to be more of a spiritual leader in your life. Or perhaps you wish she were less demanding of your time and less involved in your life.

You wish your friend would make more time for you, so you develop expectations for her to take your every call and get together for lunch once a week. You wish she were more of an encourager when you are struggling. Or you wish she would be quick to listen rather than quick to give advice.

I can come unglued and stuff hurtful thoughts all day long around this issue of relationship expectations. My retaliation rocks are usually coated with unmet expectations.

So, what do I do? Well, I've found it tremendously helpful to list the expectations I have of a relationship in which I'm feeling slighted. Then I prayerfully discern whether or not my expectations are realistic or unrealistic. And if I can't really discern one way or the other, I ask. I ask God. I ask that person. I ask someone wise who knows both of us well.

Unrealistic expectations are things the other person isn't able or willing to do for me. I have to let go of these. Certainly God can either change that person or change me by rearranging my desires.

In the meantime, it's unfair of me to use my expectations as the standard for their behavior or hold it against them when they don't live up to my hopes.

Realistic expectations are things I can reasonably expect the other person to do for me. My next step, then, is to discern how I can communicate these expectations with gentleness and in the right timing. Timing is key.

My pastor's wife, Holly Furtick, recently told me that she discerns through prayer the timing of such conversations with her husband, Steven. As she's running errands, fixing dinner, or flipping through her fashion magazines (the girl loves fashion!), she prays for God to make the timing clear. And He does!

Once she'd been wanting to talk to Steven about something that had been bothering her, but she didn't want it to become a big deal. She determined it was a realistic expectation on her part, so she committed to pray for the right timing. A few weeks later, she and Steven were coming home from a trip. Suddenly, he slid a piece of paper her way and said, "Write down three things I could do better as your husband."

Holly smiled. This was exactly what she'd been praying for— but even better! Her husband was the one who paved the way for a healthy conversation.

Why not take your expectations and your need for discernment about them to God in prayer? Why not ask Him to get involved? Holly's example inspired me and gave me yet another tool to keep me from stuffing and forming rocks of retaliation. God doesn't always work so quickly in answering our timing prayers, but what a comfort and encouragement to see how Holly's situation turned out.

Yes, it is possible to let conflicts, confrontations, and well-timed conversations lead our relationships to better places. Improved places. Places where we learn to process instead of stuff and leave the rock collecting behind. Unless, of course, you are talking about pretty, little, shiny rocks. In that case, honey, you can do all the rock collecting you want. Hint, hint Art!

Feelings

I think Morris Albert was on to something when he penned the wildly popular 1970s song "Feelings." He wrote, "Feelings—nothing more than feelings." In this brokenhearted ballad *feelings* consume everything; indeed, almost every line has the word *feelings* in it. Over and over and over, it truly is nothing more than feelings.

How like a woman's world. Whether we're dealing with exploding or stuffing, it all comes back to the raw emotions we're feeling in the moment. And those emotions can be tough. But I pray these chapters have introduced the possibility of thinking through strategies now that will help us not explode or stuff later. We must always remember that feelings should be indicators, not dictators. I know I've stated this truth before, but I need to hear things over and over before they really sink in. Another way God put this truth in front of me was while driving the car pool one morning.

One of my kids is not too fond of getting up at o'dark-hundred to get ready for school. And, no, it's not the one who last year dramatically laid herself across the front door stoop and proclaimed that making a child go to school was officially abuse.

No. It's her sister.

On the way to school on this oh-so-pleasant morning, we were having quite the bonding moment as I explained that her actions were unacceptable and would reap consequences. I love consequences. I love letting consequences scream so I don't have to. Anyhow, in the middle of this tender bonding moment, said child proclaimed, "I just don't feel like being nice some mornings. And if I don't feel nice, I can't act nice."

Feelings, nothing more than feelings.

I wish I could control the soundtrack of my life with the push of a button. I would have blared this song and used it to make a very dramatic point as we pulled up to the middle school. Instead, I looked at her and blurted out some wisdom that was so good I had to call a friend and brag immediately after I dropped off happy girl.

"Feelings are indicators, not dictators, child. They can indicate where your heart is in the moment, but that doesn't mean they have the right to dictate your behavior and boss you around. You are more than the sum total of your feelings and perfectly capable of that little gift from Jesus called self-control!"

I'm very confident the glassed-over look and the long, drawn-out "Mommmmmm" meant she totally connected with my early morning sermonette. But no matter if she did or didn't, *I* totally connected with this truth — a truth I'm fairly certain came straight from the Holy Spirit and was meant as much for me as for my daughter. Don't you just love it when you're disciplining your kids and God whispers, "This is good. I hope you're listening so you can apply this same truth to your life"?

When my emotions are in charge, I always seem to end up feeling like the person described by the prophet Jeremiah: "Cursed is the one who trusts in man, who depends on flesh for his strength and whose heart turns away from the LORD. He will be like a bush in the wastelands.... He will dwell in the parched places of the desert" (Jeremiah 17:5–6 NIV 1984). Yep, when I let my feelings boss me around and trust only in my flesh to handle situations, I turn into a crusty ol' burnt-up bush living in parched places.

God gave me more than just a heart to use in processing life. He gave me a mind as well.

Now don't get me wrong, it's good to feel. Feelings are indicators, and it's good to honestly assess what we're feeling and why. We need to keep a gauge on our hearts so we can process, clarify, and understand our lives and relationships more deeply. But God gave me more than just a heart to use in processing life. He gave me a mind as well. A mind made for truth to reign supreme and to keep my heart in check. We must remember, "The heart is deceitful above all things.... I the LORD search the heart and examine the mind" (Jeremiah 17:9–10).

We are more than just a sum total of our feelings. We are more than exploders who shame ... or exploders who blame. We are more than stuffers who build barriers ... or stuffers who collect retaliation rocks. Indeed, we are more. We are children of God made to walk in truth with soul integrity.

I Need a
Procedure Manual

If I suddenly want everyone in my house to be put on high cleaning alert, I invite a guest to stay with us. And if that guest happens to be my mama, y'all, I'm going to get a little neurotic. Not because of her coming to visit — I'm excited about that. But because I want her to see I've turned out okay, and that I'm not raising my family in a pigsty. "Pigsty" is how she always described the room I occupied as a teenager.

Ahem.

So, when my mama is coming to town, two things are an absolute must:

1. I must pluck my eyebrows.

2. I must drive down to the Target and get some new towels for her to use. I live in a five-kid, three-dog family. (Remember the towel issue from chapter 1? Need I say more?)

I had worked really hard to make sure my house was just so for Mama. I even stocked the fridge with fresh-cut fruit and made sure the dog hair had been appropriately washed out of the sheets on her bed. Just call me fancy.

Everything was going well. Mama even commented about how nice and clean my downstairs looked. Sheer bliss. Then she went upstairs to get settled into her room. Suddenly, a question I won't soon forget sailed down the staircase and rang in my ears: "Lysa, where's the toilet seat for the kids' bathroom?"

Huh?

"Why, Mama, what on earth do you mean?" Heart thumping, red-faced, and seriously confused, I ran upstairs.

Well, friends, all I can say is that there was nothing but a porcelain bowl where the toilet seat used to be. My girls are responsible for their own bathroom maintenance, so how was I supposed to know? And when I asked my kids about it, they nonchalantly said, "Oh yeah, it's been that way for about a month."

A month? Lord, help me!

And that's when I felt something inside me shift. Suddenly, my one overriding motive became to prove to my mama that I really did have it all together even though I obviously did not!

I got snippy and extra controlling with my kids for the remainder of the visit. If they forgot to say "please" or "thank you" in front of my mom, I gave them consequences way bigger than the offense. I was super critical of their every move and neurotic about being on time and organized with every detail of our two days together. And in the end, I even got short-tempered with my mom.

Yuck. Oh, how corrupted motives can really make me come unglued. By motives, I mean my desires—the feelings that drive me to act, react, and live the way I live. Mostly I'm a good person with good motives, but not always. Not when I just want life to be a little more about me or about making sure I look good. That's when my motives become corrupted.

Avoiding reality never changes reality.

The Bible is pretty blunt in naming the real issue here: evil desires.

Yikes. I don't like that term at all. And it seems a bit severe for what I was dealing with, doesn't it? But in the depths of my heart I know the truth. Avoiding reality never changes reality. Sigh. I think I should say that again: Avoiding reality never changes reality. And change is what I really want.

So, upon the table I now place my honesty: I have evil desires.

I do.

Maybe not the kind that will land me on some sort of *48 Hours Mystery* episode, but the kind that pull me away from the kind of woman I want to be. One with a calm spirit and divine nature. I want it to be evident that I know Jesus, love Jesus, and spend time with Jesus each day. So why do other things bubble to the surface when my life gets stressful and my relationships get strained? Things like . . .

> *Selfishness:* I want things my way.
>
> *Pride:* I see things only from my vantage point.
>
> *Impatience:* I rush things without proper consideration.
>
> *Anger:* I let simmering frustrations erupt.
>
> *Bitterness:* I swallow eruptions and let them fester.

It's easier to avoid these realities than to deal with them. I'd much rather deal with my junk drawers than deal with the junk in my heart. I'd much rather run to the mall and get a new shirt than run to God and get a new attitude. I'd much rather dig into a brownie than dig into my heart. I'd much rather point the finger at other people's issues than take a peek at my own. Plus, it's just a whole lot easier to clean my junk drawers, run to the store, eat a brownie, and look at other people's issues. A whole lot easier.

I rationalize that I don't have time to get all psychological and examine my selfishness, pride, impatience, anger, and bitterness. And honestly, I'm tired of knowing I have issues but having no clue how to rein them in on a given day. I need something simple. A quick reality check I can remember in the midst of the everyday messies.

And sister, I think I found just that.

Positioning My Heart
in the Flow of God's Power

Remember our chapter 3 discussion of Peter? The apostle who changed from shifty to rock solid? Oh, how I relate to this man. I often find myself reading the two letters in the New Testament that bear his name. Although there is scholarly debate about whether or not Peter actually wrote 2 Peter, it seems clear that whoever did write it understood the struggle of wanting to be one way but acting another; having divine power but falling prey to evil desires; knowing and loving Jesus but sometimes feeling ineffective and unproductive in living out that reality.

Do I hear a sister sigh in agreement? Maybe a little whispered, "Me too"?

Good gracious, laying this honesty on the table is hard, isn't it? But I love these verses from 2 Peter that so clearly address my issues:

> His divine power has given us everything we need for a godly life through our knowledge of him who called us by his own glory and goodness. Through these he has given us his very great and precious promises, so that through them you may participate in the divine nature, having escaped the corruption in the world caused by evil desires.
>
> For this very reason, make every effort to add to your faith goodness; and to goodness, knowledge; and to knowledge, self-control; and to self-control, perseverance; and to perseverance, godliness; and to godliness, mutual affection; and to mutual affection, love. For if you possess these qualities in increasing

measure, they will keep you from being ineffective and unproductive in your knowledge of our Lord Jesus Christ. (2 Peter 1:3–8)

Wow. God's divine power has given us everything we need for a godly life? *Everything?* If that's the case, why do I still come unglued?

Yes, God has given us everything, but I'm learning that this promise comes with a requirement. I have to "make every effort" to add some things to my faith. Things like goodness, knowledge, and self-control. I have to add these in. I have to make that choice. Then I can position my heart in the flow of God's power and work with it rather than against it.

It is through God's "great and precious promises" that I can participate in the divine nature. A nature very different from my own. I may not be gentle by nature, but I can be gentle by obedience. If—and only if—I equip myself with predetermined biblical procedures that I can rely on when I start to feel the great unglued coming on.

> *I may not be gentle by nature, but I can be gentle by obedience.*

I recently experienced a vivid illustration of how crucial it is to have predetermined procedures. I had taken my seat on a flight to a speaking engagement. Everything seemed to be quite normal during the rest of the boarding process. But as the plane was about to taxi, things got very abnormal. A woman just a few rows behind me started screaming obscenities. And when I say screaming, I don't mean talking too loudly. I mean full-out vocal extremes.

She was completely undone because she found a piece of chewed gum stuck to her bag of chips. Where the gum came from was a mystery, but how she felt about that gum was not. What came out of her mouth was so R-rated it made my already wide eyes pop out like a bug on steroids.

She was so loud and out of control that the flight attendants quickly alerted the captain to abort the flight. When it became obvious the flight attendants were not going to be able to contain the situation either, two plainly dressed men on the plane suddenly stood and flashed federal marshal badges.

And just as a side note, I don't know how you get one of those badges, but I'm totally into it. I suddenly had visions of being one of Charlie's Angels, flashing a badge, doing high karate kicks, and subduing the bad guys. Or, in this case, one screaming woman. Seriously, if this speaking and writing thing doesn't work out, I'm going to get a badge of some sort.

Anyhow. One of the marshals gathered the flight crew while the other tried to talk down the passenger. Every airline professional on board immediately went into by-the-book mode. It was clear they had been well trained on how to handle crazy situations. They didn't get emotional. They simply followed procedures. I watched in amazement as the woman kept escalating her wild behavior, but the people trained to handle her never did.

She screamed.

They talked in calm, hushed tones.

She threatened.

They deflected her threats with gentle warnings.

Then she took things to a whole new level: "I have a bomb! I have a bomb! I have a bomb!"

I am not kidding.

I know you think I am. But I am not.

That's when I pulled out the anointing oil my pastor had given to me the day before. My seat became oily and holy. I called Art and my friend Amy and asked them to pray. And I tweeted, asking my cyber friends to pray.

Eventually, the marshals — along with two policemen and additional Homeland Security people who'd boarded the plane — handcuffed her and removed her from the flight.

I will be honest with you: This woman took unglued to a level I will never forget and hope never to experience again. But I also never want to forget the incredible responses of the flight attendants and officers who dealt with this explosive situation. Not only did their obviously thorough training and procedures keep them calm, they kept an entire planeload of passengers calm as well. And that was an amazing thing to behold.

So, I started thinking that maybe I needed my own set of default procedures for when selfishness, pride, impatience, anger, or bitterness rear their ugly heads. Because in the moment I feel them, I feel justified in feeling them and find them hard to battle. But God's promises — His truths and examples from Scripture — are powerful enough to redirect me to the divine nature I'm meant to have. Having a predetermined plan from Him will help me stay calmer when I start to feel unglued. More godly. More in line with Scripture.

I need my own set of default procedures for when selfishness, pride, impatience, anger, or bitterness rear their ugly heads.

Sure, I will still be vulnerable to coming unglued. Even after reading this book, you will too. Every one of us is susceptible to unpredictable emotions, hormonally influenced emotions. That being said, I still want to equip myself in every way possible to stay out of the emotional fray. I want to stay in the flow of God's power and participate in His divine nature.

My Biblical Procedure Manual

One of my favorite Old Testament examples of how to handle raw emotions is King Jehoshaphat, whose story is told in 2 Chronicles 20. One day this king got some very bad news. Three countries had banded together, forming a massive army to attack his much smaller country of Judah. Danger was thick. Defeat seemed imminent. Death on a massive scale was a looming reality.

I think I might have felt just the teeniest bit unglued under the circumstances, wouldn't you? Yet, in the face of this potentially horrific situation, King Jehoshaphat didn't freak out or explode. Instead, he did five specific things that gave me a whole new perspective on how to hold myself together when a life event threatens to blow me apart. Based on the truths in Jehoshaphat's story, I outlined a training plan for my heart and mind and wrote a predetermined biblical procedure manual to bring godly calm to my own unglued situations.

STEP 1: **Remember who you are.**

> Alarmed, Jehoshaphat resolved to inquire of the LORD, and he proclaimed a fast for all Judah. The people of Judah came together to seek help from the LORD; indeed, they came from every town in Judah to seek him. (2 Chronicles 20:3–4)

I love the way this story states from the beginning that Jehoshaphat had feelings of alarm. Given the situation, alarm was an appropriate feeling. However, while his feeling was a valid and reasonable indicator of what he was facing, it didn't force him into an unglued reaction. Why? Because the Scriptures are clear he had already predetermined how he'd respond. The two words that immediately precede and follow King Jehoshaphat's name — *alarmed* and *resolved* — represent two realities that are especially significant for this struggle I have with raw emotions.

Alarmed, Jehoshaphat *resolved*. The king had *resolved* to inquire of the Lord. This is how I want to be. When I feel alarmed, I want simultaneously to be resolved. *Alarmed*, Lysa *resolved*. And here's what I want to be resolved to do — to remember who I am.

We have a four-word family motto we say to our kids almost every time they step out the door of our home. These four words encapsulate every moral lesson, every biblical lesson, and every life lesson we've taught them. We repeat this phrase instead of blasting them with a sermonette: "Be nice, use your manners, watch your words, don't drink, don't smoke, don't drive over the speed limit," and on and on. Instead, all they get are four words:

Remember who you are.

This means: Remember, you are a TerKeurst, and a good name is better than all the riches of the world. And even more importantly than that, remember you are a child of God, holy and dearly loved, whom God has set apart for a mighty plan. There ain't nothing in this world worth trading all that for. Indeed, remember who you are.

King Jehoshaphat was resolved. He predetermined to remember who he was. And it prevented him from coming unglued. I need to do the very same thing. I'm not an unglued woman who is a slave to her circumstances, her hormones, or to other people's attitudes. Those things might affect me, but they don't rule me. I am a child of God, holy and dearly loved, whom God has set apart for a mighty plan. And there ain't nothing in this world worth trading all that for. Indeed, I must remember who I am.

STEP 2: Redirect your focus to Jesus.

> For we have no power to face this vast army that is attacking us. We do not know what to do, but our eyes are upon you.
> (2 Chronicles 20:12 NIV 1984)

Isn't it frustrating to be in situations, conflicts, or hard places and have no idea what to do? It's hard when we feel like there are no easy solutions and no certain answers. But I love the honest admission by King Jehoshaphat and his people. They didn't know what to do, but they knew *who* to turn to. Their attention was fixed on the Lord. I have relied on the truth of this verse many times over when I didn't know what to do.

A few years ago, I was nearing the end of a conference at which I'd been speaking, and I was looking forward to a relaxing dinner with our team that night. My friend Beth and I were talking about potential restaurant choices when a frantic arena staff member told us there was an emergency and we were needed right away. A woman attending the conference had just been told her two grandchildren had been killed that day in a fire. Moments later we were at the side of a woman lying on the floor, surrounded by her friends and sobbing to the point she could hardly breathe.

The woman's grandbabies, ages eight and four, had recently spent spring break with her. Just days earlier, she'd held them, rocked them, stroked their hair, and kissed them all over their faces. How could they be gone? The tragic news was too much for her to process, and she'd collapsed.

The EMT who'd been trying to help her breathe stepped aside so we could hold the woman's hands and pray with her. At first, I stumbled my way through requests for Jesus to pour His most tender mercies into this situation. I prayed for comfort and the reassurance that these precious children were being held by Jesus at that very moment. It was so hard. My mommy heart ached deeply for this woman, and I couldn't contain my own tears.

As my friend Beth began to pray, I noticed something miraculous. Every time she said "Jesus," the woman's body relaxed, her crying slowed, and her breathing eased. So, when it was my turn to pray again, I just said His name over and over and over. This sweet grandmother joined me, "Jesus, Jesus, Jesus."

As we continued to repeat the name of Jesus, we felt an outpouring of power beyond what we were capable of mustering up on our own. The Bible teaches that there is power and protection in the Lord's name (John 17:11). I saw that power. I experienced it. And I won't soon forget it.

The human soul is designed to recognize and respond to the

calm assurance of Jesus. When I am in an unglued place, I can invite a power beyond my own into the situation by simply speaking His name. I don't have to know what to do. I don't have to have all the answers. I don't have to remember everything I learned in Bible study last week. I just have to remember one thing, one name —Jesus.

And this isn't something that applies only to the tragic events of life. It applies to the everyday ones as well. Sometimes I'll be driving the kids to school in the morning, determined that we are all going to be nice and act godly. Sometimes I'll even get a wild hair and dare to do a little devotion as part of our commute. But then everyone starts bumping into my happy and wham! Mama is no longer in the mood for devotions. Mama is in the mood to yell.

I've been known in a moment like that to grab the steering wheel and just start proclaiming out loud, "Jesus ... Jesus ... Jesus ... Jesus ... Jesus." I invite His power right into my little carpooling vehicle! And it completely wigs out my kids. They've been known to say, "Mama, please don't roll down the window when you pull up to school, okay?"

Yes, keeping my eyes and my mouth focused on Jesus is a crucial part of my unglued procedure manual.

STEP 3: **Recognize God's job isn't your job.**

"Listen, King Jehoshaphat and all who live in Judah and Jerusalem! This is what the LORD says to you: 'Do not be afraid or discouraged because of this vast army. For the battle is not yours, but God's.'" (2 Chronicles 20:15)

Sometimes I get into situations where I'm consumed with trying to figure out what to do. The more I think through options, the more the unglued feelings come. Have you ever been in that frustrating place? Maybe you're there right now. That's why this verse is so encouraging. Ultimately, the responsibility for winning this battle we're facing doesn't belong to us. We're not responsible for figuring it all out. *Our job* is simply to be obedient to God in the midst of what we're facing. *God's job* is results. Obedience positions us in the flow of God's power, working with God's ways instead of against God's ways.

Are you overwhelmed by money issues? Look up verses on money and start applying God's Word to your bank account and your bills. The issues may not change at first, but over time your heart will change. God honors the heart that honors Him.

Having marital problems? Look up biblical truths addressed to husbands and wives and start applying them. Determine to be the spouse God is calling you to be. I know this is hard, but I also know it has worked wonders in helping me stay in the flow of God's power.

Dealing with friendship troubles? Same thing. Search the pages of Scripture and ground yourself in teaching about words and how we use them with each other. Practice staying in the flow of God's power by keeping your words in line with God's truth. Again, not easy but absolutely transforming.

I learned a great lesson about staying in the flow at a family camp last summer. Tucked away in the Adirondack Mountains of New York, Camp-of-the-Woods is an amazing getaway — great chapel preaching every morning, no TV, crystal-clear lake, campfires, fishing, putt-putt golf, shuffleboard, and more game playing than you can imagine. It's also an incredibly beautiful location with numerous scenic views and walking trails. So when some exercise-loving friends suggested we join them for a moderate family hike, we thought that was a great idea.

Well, it turns out their definition of *moderate* came from an entirely different dictionary than mine. Actually, an entirely different planet, if I'm being completely honest. Honey, honey, honey ... this was no *moderate* hike.

I had pictured a path with a gently winding, upward slope. But what we actually experienced was more like scaling a cliff face made entirely of rocks and roots.

Not kidding.

And we were at an altitude so high my lungs felt like they were stuck together and incapable of holding more than a thimbleful of breath. Lovely. And forget having any type of conversation. All I could do was mutter a few moans between my gasps for air.

Up, up, up we went. And when another group of hikers passed us on their way down and cheerfully quipped, "You're almost halfway there!" I wanted to quit. *Halfway?* How could we only be halfway?!

I pushed. I pulled. I strained. I huffed and puffed. And I might have even spent a few minutes pouting. But eventually, we reached the top. I bent over, holding my sides and wondering how a girl who runs four miles almost every day of her life could feel so stinkin' out of shape!

Climbing up the mountain against the force of gravity was hard. Really, really hard. But coming down was a completely different experience. I navigated the same rocks and roots without feeling nearly as stressed. I enjoyed the journey. I noticed more of the beautiful surroundings and had enough breath to actually talk all the way down.

About halfway down the trail, it occurred to me how similar my experience of this hike was to my Christian walk. Starting at the top of the mountain and working *with* the force of gravity was so much easier than starting at the bottom of the mountain and working *against* it. Although I had to navigate the exact same path both directions, being in the flow of gravity made the journey so much better.

It's just like when I face a hard issue in life. Operating *in the flow* of God's power is so much better than working *against the flow* of God's power. Seeking to obey God in the midst of whatever circumstance I'm facing is what positions me to work in the flow of God's power. I still have to navigate the realities of my situation, but I won't be doing it in my own strength. My job is to be obedient to God, to apply His Word, and to walk according to His ways — not according to the world's suggestions. I want to participate in His divine nature rather than wallow in my own bad attitude and insecurities.

Operating in the flow of God's power is so much better than working against it.

Then I won't have to huff and puff and pout while trying to figure everything out on my own. I stay in the flow. God, in His way and timing, works it all out.

That's what happened with King Jehoshaphat. I'm sure if he had tried to figure out how to win this battle based on his limited strength and numbers alone, he would have surely given up. Judah was outnumbered. No question. But instead of counting themselves out, the king and his army counted God in and determined to do exactly as He instructed — even when what God instructed must have seemed like three shades of crazy.

STEP 4: Recite thanks and praises to God.

> After consulting the people, Jehoshaphat appointed men to sing to the LORD and to praise him for the splendor of his holiness as they went out at the head of the army, saying: "Give thanks to the LORD, for his love endures forever." (2 Chronicles 20:21)

I don't know about you, but if I had been facing certain death at the hands of a marauding horde, my first line of defense would not have been to send out the choir.

Oh, if only I were more in the habit of having a thankful heart full of praises instead of a grumbling heart consumed with circumstances. The hard thing is, I just don't feel very thankful in that moment when problems start bumping into my happy. I just don't feel like busting out in a praise song. I wish I did. But I don't.

So, in the midst of an unglued moment, how do I shift from *having an attitude* to *walking in gratitude*? I need a go-to script that will redirect my perspective to a better place. And I think I have just the thing. I say out loud to myself, "If this is the worst thing that happens to me today, it's still a pretty good day."

My friend just hurt my feelings. If this is the worst thing that happens to me today, it's still a pretty good day. Praise You, God.

My husband is running late at work, and now I have to stay with the kids and miss the fun girls' night out I'd been planning to attend. If this is the worst thing that happens to me today, it's still a pretty good day. Praise You, God.

My Bible study leader just asked Stacey to fill in for her next week when I've often told her, "I'd love to do that sometime." If this is the worst thing that happens to me today, it's still a pretty good day. Praise You, God.

I can't authentically praise God for anything that is wrong or evil, but I sure can shift my focus to all that is right and praise Him for that. And in the story of King Jehoshaphat, making this shift—from looking at what was wrong to praising God for what was right—worked a miracle.

When the praise chorus from Judah's front line of defense reached the ears of the opposing armies, these enemies were so confused that rather than fight against Judah they started fighting among themselves instead. And "when the men of Judah came to the place that overlooks the desert and looked toward the vast army, they saw only dead bodies lying on the ground; no one had escaped" (2 Chronicles 20:24). Amazing! Absolutely amazing.

Oh, how powerful it is to shift from an attitude to gratitude and to praise our God in the midst of it all. When I do this, my circumstances may not instantly change, but the way I look at those circumstances certainly does. I stop being blind to all that's right and see so many more reasons to praise God. And when my heart is full of praise, my emotions aren't nearly as prone to coming unglued!

STEP 5: Realize reactions determine reach.

> The fear of God came upon all the surrounding kingdoms when they heard how the LORD had fought against the enemies of Israel. And the kingdom of Jehoshaphat was at peace, for his God had given him rest on every side. (2 Chronicles 20:29–30)

How did Jehoshaphat find peace? Why did he have rest on every side? And most importantly, why did the fear of God come upon all who heard about Jehoshaphat's victory? Because in the midst of it all, he honored God with his actions and reactions.

Remember, though he was alarmed, he was resolved to inquire of the Lord.

He felt alarmed but stayed resolved. He kept his focus on the Lord. He stayed in the flow of God's power by being obedient to God's Word. Though it wasn't easy, he shifted from having an attitude to practicing gratitude. And his reaction positively affected everyone around him, not only people in his own kingdom, but even those in surrounding countries. This is the kind of leader I want to follow. This is the kind of leader I want to be. Not that I'm leading a kingdom, but I *am* influencing the people around me. The interactions I have with my kids, my husband, my friends, my neighbors, my church, even the checkout clerk at my local grocery store — they matter. My reactions testify to the kind of relationship I have with Jesus and the effect He has on my heart. After all, I'm reminded in the Bible that out of the overflow of the heart the mouth speaks. When my happy gets bumped, what's really going on in my heart is on display. In those times I will either add to the authenticity of my love for Jesus or, sadly, negate it.

Yes, my reactions determined my reach. That's why when I feel the great unglued coming on, I want to train my mind to remember each step, each truth, each choice Jehoshaphat made. Then I want to train my heart to have the courage to implement each one.

So, here's the short version of my predetermined biblical procedure manual all in one place:

1. Alarmed, I resolve to remember who I am.
2. Jesus, Jesus, Jesus.
3. Stay in the flow — my job is obedience; God's job is results.
4. Shift from an attitude to gratitude.
5. My reactions determine my reach.

Instead of avoiding the reality that I come unglued, I'm tackling it head-on. I want to give myself every fighting chance to make wise choices in the midst of raw emotions. And having a predetermined plan is a good thing to create and implement. Care to join me? Not that your plan will look the same as mine. Feel free to take this idea and make it your own. The best kind of plan for you is the one you'll follow.

And if we ever get to have a face-to-face chat, I'd love to hear what you come up with. I bet we'd have a grand time swapping stories about our imperfect progress. I can't promise if you come to my house I'll have a proper toilet seat to sit on, but I can promise if someone invites us on a hike I'll require pictures first. Okay?

My Kid-Placemat Life

My goal in processing unglued reactions is to pull the swings of my emotional pendulum back from the extremes of the ugly unglued and keep them swaying in the gentle middle. Finding the gentle middle between exploding and stuffing can be hard, but God is working on me. How about you?

Certainly, identifying our tendencies is a great start. And developing strategies to process and diffuse emotions without stuffing and exploding, as we did in the preceding chapters, is crucial. But there's yet another layer we must add before we move on. It's perspective.

Perspective calls forth a gentleness I can't seem to find any other way. And lately I've had this Bible verse chasing me around: "Let your gentleness be evident to all" (Philippians 4:5). I've run across this verse in so many unexpected places that I know it's something God wants me to pay attention to. Why? Let's just say, when the Lord was handing out the gentleness gene in July of 1969, I was apparently in another line waiting for something else. Lots of people who were being fashioned at the same time did get the gentleness gene. I know some people who I'm sure stood in line twice and got a double portion. Me? Not so much.

Now, I can have moments of gentleness. I can perform acts of gentleness. But gentleness doesn't ooze from the core of who I am. This is especially true if I am sleepy or stressed. Honestly, I think I need one of those warning signs on the bedroom door to enter at your own risk after 8:30 p.m.: "DANGER! Please note that the Holy Spirit has temporarily left this woman's body to go help a sister half-way around the world who is just now waking up."

Now, I know that is some terrible theology, but I'm being honest, ya'll. What little threads of gentleness I do have are not evident past 8:30 p.m. Not. At. All.

And then there is this thing that happens when I get stressed. Normally, I can pull off a little gentleness throughout the day, but throw in a stressful situation where too much is coming at me too quickly and mercy lou! I get task-oriented and start talking in a staccato-like cadence to my people, because I want the stuff around the house done. right. now. not. in. ten. minutes. because. now. means. now!

I don't want this to be how my kids remember me. Staccato mama.

I don't want this to be how I remember me in this season of life.

So, this Philippians verse that has been nipping at the edges of my heart and mind, about letting my gentleness be evident to all, is something I know I need—even if it does sting a bit.

Here's a little sermon I've been preaching to myself: Let your gentleness be evident to all. The "your" part means I do have some. Much as I'd like to believe otherwise, God didn't skip over me in distributing the gentleness gene, and my wildfire personality isn't a divine exception. Regardless of the stress I'm under, I am capable of displaying God's gentleness because the Holy Spirit is in me. I have the Holy Spirit in me when I feel all chipper at 8:30 a.m., and I have the Holy Spirit in me when I feel grumpy at 8:30 p.m. The Spirit is in me when I feel calm and when I feel stressed. Gentleness is in me!

I just have to learn to reclaim the gentleness that is rightfully mine. And I can reclaim it by practicing the one word that appears right before, "Let your gentleness be evident to all" (Philippians 4:5). That little word is *rejoice*: "Rejoice in the Lord always. I will say it again: Rejoice!" (Philippians 4:4). The more my heart is parked in a place of thanksgiving and rejoicing, the less room I have for grumpiness.

The more my heart is parked in a place of thanksgiving and rejoicing, the less room I have for grumpiness.

My kids are driving me crazy? At least they are healthy enough to have that kind of energy. Don't miss this chance to rejoice.

My laundry is piled to the ceiling? Every stitch of clothing is evidence of life in my home. Don't miss this chance to rejoice.

My husband isn't all skippy romantic about the two of us shopping together? In the grand scheme of life, so what? He's a good man. Don't miss this chance to rejoice.

I feel unorganized and behind and late on everything? Scale back, let unrealistic expectations go, and savor some happy moments today. Don't miss this chance to rejoice.

The more I rejoice, the more I keep things in perspective. The more I keep things in perspective, the gentler I become.

That's why I have to intentionally seek out perspective-magnifying opportunities. Things like serving at a soup kitchen, delivering gifts to a family in need, or going on a mission trip. If I want the gentleness inside me to be unleashed, I have to break away from my everyday routine. I have to go where perspective awaits me.

Reevaluating My Kid-Placemat Life

When my girls were little, we had a love-hate relationship with those paper placemats some fast food restaurants use to entertain kids. I loved that the placemats featured appealing, attention-grabbing pictures and came with complimentary crayons. However, it never failed that someone would color on someone else's placemat and squeals and screams would have all heads in the restaurant turning our way.

Then I would sit there in disbelief that my kids had caused such a fuss over colored-on placemats. Placemats that would soon be covered in ketchup and juice and eventually tossed in the trash. Fleeting things. Insignificant things. I knew my kids wouldn't even remember the placemats tomorrow, let alone a month from now. But for today, this moment, the placemats had them coming all unglued.

And I'm no different. If I carefully consider some of the stuff I come unglued over, I honestly must shake my head. Not to shame myself, but to wake myself up and realize that there are legitimate things that warrant my mental energy. Is this situation I'm facing today really one of those things?

I thought about those placemats recently ... and at the strangest time. I was in Los Angeles with some of my friends volunteering at the Dream Center. Pastor Matthew Barnett and his church run this amazing place, which is a ministry hub of 120 programs that serve more than 40,000 people every month. Housed in a converted hospital building, the 700-bed facility includes a transitional shelter for homeless families, a drug rehab center, and a shelter for victims of sex trafficking. The center also offers educational development programs that train participants in job skills and provides life-skills counseling to homeless families and individuals.

We decided to forgo staying at a hotel so we could live at the homeless shelter for the five days we would spend volunteering there. I knew perspective would be waiting for me at the Dream Center. And it was.

On our first day, we served food at a soup kitchen on Skid Row —one of the outreach ministries of the Dream Center. I saw so many people in such desperate situations I had a hard time processing it all. There were prostitutes, pimps, people high on who knows what, heaps of trash being used for beds, and makeshift tents on the sidewalk.

I watched a crack deal take place just a few feet away from us—two people, right out in the open, who made no attempt to conceal what they were doing. And we were literally just around the corner from a police station.

Drugs. Propositions. Homelessness. Filth. Darkness. This is where we were. And this is what I couldn't understand: *Why do they stay?*

The Dream Center sends resources to this dark corner of Los Angeles several times a week. They bring food but, perhaps even more important than physical sustenance, they also bring hope. Hope for something more, something new, a chance for a different life.

But very few ever leave Skid Row.

Comfort zones are like that. Remember, comfort zones don't have to be comfortable—they're just familiar. It's where you feel like you belong. And where you come to believe you belong is where you will stay.

I saw this sad refusal to break out of the Skid-Row life in a woman I met that day named Janice. Janice listened to our promises that the people at the Dream Center could help her detox, give her a safe place to stay, and get her back on her feet. And I thought she truly believed us.

We helped Janice into the rescue van, drove away from Skid Row, checked her into the rehab floor at the Dream Center, and left feeling relieved and full of hope for her. We were so happy she was willing to get help.

The next day, we were working in a different part of Los Angeles when a woman asking for money approached me and my friend, Amanda. I thought the woman looked familiar, but it took my brain a few seconds to figure out how I knew her. Then it hit me—it was Janice, my friend from Skid Row. Why was she here? She wasn't supposed to be here. She was supposed to be in the drug rehab program at the Dream Center where we'd checked her in the day before. But she'd walked away less than twenty-four hours later. Away from help. Away from hope. Away from restoration.

And here she was, begging for money to buy a bus ticket to get back to Skid Row. In a city of nearly four million people, somehow our paths had crossed again. What are the odds? Surely, it was a sign of how much God cared for her.

"Oh Janice, why did you leave the Dream Center?" I asked. "Can I take you back? I can call for a Dream Center bus to come get you right now. Please, please let's go back."

But Janice just shook her head and quietly whispered, "I have to go back to the streets 'cause I know where to put my blankets there. I don't know where to put my blankets anywhere else."

"Back to Skid Row?" I asked, tears in my eyes. She nodded. And I knew she wouldn't let us take her back to the Dream Center. Not that day. Maybe not ever. As much as my heart ached to force this rescue, I knew I couldn't rob Janice of one of the only things she possessed — her choice. She had to want to go with us. And that's not what she wanted.

I asked if we might pray for her. She agreed. We circled and prayed and then watched her walk away and approach another person for money. And then another. Rejected most of the time. But slowly walking away, away, away.

There are times I am no more mature than my kids arguing over throwaway placemats.

That was the strange moment I thought of those stupid placemats — the ones the kids fought over. And my anger burned. Not at my kids, but at myself and all the dumb things I can get bent out of shape about. There are times I am no more mature than my kids arguing over throwaway placemats. How dare I get angry over things so inconsequential. God, forgive me.

Yes, there are things that *should* make me angry. Like Janice not knowing her whole life that she could put her blankets somewhere safe. And now the place she keeps returning to is Skid Row. "Heroin Alley" on Skid Row, to be exact. Where pimps sell women to do unspeakable things in makeshift tents right on the street. And where kids play with dirty needles and teens pass out with needles in their toes because the veins in their arms and legs are too abused to shoot drugs.

There are reasonable things to be angry about today, but not slight inconveniences and little things that bump into my happy. God help me and my kid-placemat life.

Yes, perspective was there at the Dream Center. I went as a woman in ministry. I went to help meet needs. But I also quickly realized I was there as a woman in need. A woman who needed God's reality to fall fresh and heavy and close and real and too in-my-face to deny. Because sometimes I find myself talking about God so much He becomes more of an *identity marker* than an *identity changer* in my life.

Having God as an identity marker reduces Him to nothing more than a label, a lingo, and a lifestyle—I'm a Christian so I talk like one and act like one. But having God as an identity changer is much, much more. It means I am no longer the person I was before, someone who comes unglued at minor things. I am making imperfect progress. Shifting, breaking away, and being chiseled. I am a woman whose identity has been changed by coming face to face with the One who has the power to completely transform me.

I saw God's identity-changing power woven into the fabric of so many lives at the Dream Center. I saw it. Oh God, how I saw it. And wanted it.

God's identity-changing power is what transformed the gang member with eight bullet hole scars into a Jesus-loving servant. So gentle.

It's what changed the prostitute into a counselor for other girls rescued from life on the streets. So pure.

It's what changed the drug addict into a loving father, teaching his son how to be a godly leader. So integrity-filled.

What in heavens was holding me back?

Seriously.

What prevented me from realizing that God's power could change me too?

I needed to know, and I felt almost desperate to figure it out.

So, I asked Pastor Matthew, "Aren't you afraid sometimes? Aren't you afraid to rely on God's power? You run a facility where you have to raise a half-million dollars a month—a *month*! Do you walk around with the weight of that on you all the time?"

His answer cracked my heart wide open.

"No," he said. "When you experience God the way I've been experiencing God for seventeen years, you stop being afraid. I've seen too many miracles."

Oh! Tears. The woman who only lets tears sting and barely brim before blinking them away felt a crack in the dam of her soul and was flooded with tears.

My. God. That. Is. It.

I've stopped positioning my life for miracles.

Somewhere along the line I stopped expecting God to work miraculously in me.

In relation to my unglued struggles, somewhere along the line I stopped expecting God to work miraculously in me. And I realized that this was yet another benefit of intentionally pursuing perspective-magnifying opportunities. For it's in such situations, when God's power is evident, that I start to believe I can experience that power in my own life. Maybe, just maybe, I can change too.

And maybe I'm not so different from Janice. Remember the

question I was wrestling with on that first day at the Dream Center: "Why do they stay?"

Comfort zones are like that. Remember, comfort zones don't have to be comfortable — they're just familiar. It's where you feel like you belong. And where you come to believe you belong is where you will stay. For too long I've believed a lie just like Janice. I've come to believe I belong in an unglued state. All the raw emotions I've stuffed. All the raw emotions I've spewed. And all the lies I've believed that I will always be this way.

But I don't have to be this way. And right in the middle of a homeless shelter, my soul quickened to the bold reality that I could be different. I really could have different reactions to my raw emotions. I knew my progress would be imperfect, but it could still be miraculous. And I felt the fresh breezes of new hope wafting through me.

I can be gentle. I can be patient. I can be peaceful. I'm not gentle by nature, but I can be gentle by obedience. I'm not patient by nature, but I can be patient by obedience. I'm not peaceful by nature, but I can be peaceful by obedience. I can. And I will. I can be the unglued woman made gentle, patient, and peaceful. God, help me. God, forgive me.

I got a huge and healthy dose of perspective at the Dream Center. And it's a good thing because it was quickly tested when I got home and discovered I'd been robbed.

Vanished

I don't have a lot of nice jewelry. Usually, you'll only find me wearing my wedding ring and another ring Art gave me for our fifteenth wedding anniversary. Other than those two rings, I have only a few simple pieces that have been given to me over the years. Little treasures not worth a lot of money, but special because they hold a lot of memories.

A child's ring my stepdad gave me the day he asked my mom to marry him.

A ring I got for my college graduation.

A bracelet my mom gave me for Christmas several years ago. And another bracelet Art gave me for Valentine's Day this year.

A legacy ring given to me the day my first daughter was born.

My college sorority pin.

A baby's signet ring, with the faint initials of my dad, who left and never came back.

Simple but special.

The morning after I returned from the Dream Center, I noticed that the bracelet Art had given me for Valentine's Day wasn't where I thought I'd left it. I spent several days searching and wondering where I'd put it. Convinced I'd simply misplaced it and would find it soon, I wasn't too worried.

When I still hadn't found it after three days, it dawned on me that maybe I'd put it in a drawer where I keep my other jewelry. I opened the drawer and my heart sank. Everything was gone. The rings. The bracelets. The pin. The one possession in this world I had that connected me to my biological father.

My first reaction was to grab both of my ring fingers. Much to my relief, I was wearing my wedding and anniversary rings. They were safe. But everything else had vanished.

I sat down on a little stool in my bathroom and willed my tired mind to make a mental list of reasons to be thankful. Okay, let's be honest, I wanted to come completely unglued and kick into aggressive figure-it-out mode. But I knew I needed to find Dream Center-type perspective in that moment. And I knew that the only thing I could do to turn my attitude around was to make a gratitude list.

Trust me, many other lists were begging to take up real estate in my brain. A list of suspects. A list of memories and how irreplaceable most of those pieces were. A list of when this might have happened and how. A list of anything else that might be missing.

But sometimes refusing to come unglued is the only way to prove to ourselves it is possible to have a different kind of reaction. A reaction where I remember the power of God is in me; therefore the power of God is accessible to me. I just have to put my heart in a position to tap into it. And the best way to position my heart to tap into the power of God is gratitude. Gratitude diffuses attitude. So, I willed those other lists aside. After all, I'd already

> *Sometimes refusing to come unglued is the only way to prove to ourselves it is possible to have a different kind of reaction.*

had enough taken from me in that moment. I didn't need to freely hand over my heart as well. And so I began my list ...

I am thankful for my children who are here and not taken.

I am thankful for my husband who will let me stick my cold feet underneath his legs tonight.

I am thankful for today's sun that shines and the moon whose light will dance with tonight's shadows.

I am thankful for the thousands of steady breaths I take every day and never have to think about.

I am thankful for memories that flicker and ignite on command.

I am thankful to still be able to retrieve those memories.

And on and on I went, until I could get up from the stool, calmly close the drawer, and ask God for just one thing. Okay, two things...

First, Lord, wrap Your hope around the person who took these things of mine right now and show them another way. They must be in a really bad spot. Come near them. And secondly, if possible, might they just return that one thing? Lord, You know what that one thing is. If possible ... and if not ... thank You still a thousand times over. For, even in the midst of things stolen, I have been given a great gift—remembering all I still have.

Perspective. It does change everything.

Perspective-magnifying opportunities such as living at the Dream Center are good for my heart. They are good for my soul. Maybe you can't travel to the Dream Center or live in your local homeless shelter for a week. That's okay. There are other perspective-magnifying opportunities all around you. What about getting involved at a local nursing home, the pediatric cancer ward, the soup kitchen, a school in an underprivileged neighborhood? For that matter, why not volunteer in your neighborhood elementary school where kids who need tutoring and help with reading are plentiful? What about the outreach programs at your church?

The place you go doesn't matter as much as the need you choose to see and meet. When we place ourselves in situations where things seem impossible, we see the hand of God in action. When we can attribute good only to God's power, we see Him in a new light and we believe in His power afresh.

Despite the demands of an overwhelming budget, an overwhelming need, and an overwhelming assignment, Pastor Matthew Barnett and his team have no other answers for how things are going to work out except the absolute certainty that the power of God will step in.

When discouragement looks close, God's power moves in closer. Where human finances, strategies, and programs fall short, God's power fills the gap. When discouragement looms close, God's power moves in closer. When people in the program drop out and the Dream Center team starts to wonder if it's possible for any of the people they serve to change, God's power works a miracle in another unlikely-to-change life.

They see God. And when I was there, I did too.

The gift I got was perspective on how blessed I am and how my problems really do pale in comparison. But I also experienced a fresh working of God's power. It's real. It's real for the people at the Dream Center. It's real for the people on Skid Row. And it's real for the unglued woman and her kid-placemat life as well.

The Empty Woman

Sometimes my unglued feelings come in a roar of stinging conversations and runaway emotions. Other times I get the great unglued when my thoughts entangle around what she has and I don't. And the *she* I'm talking about could be anyone—a friend, neighbor, or picture in a magazine. I stand in front of the mirror and all I see is what's lacking. What I am not. What I don't have. What I can't do.

Then I think of her. Who she is. What she has. What she can do. And it all just splits me open like a plow cutting a line in the soil to sow seed. Scripture warns where this thinking leads: "You will always harvest what you plant. Those who live only to satisfy their own sinful nature will harvest decay and death from that sinful nature. But those who live to please the Spirit will harvest everlasting life from the Spirit" (Galatians 6:7–8 NLT).

I know this. And yet I still drop the seeds of comparison into the furrows of my soul—seeds that grow a plant called coveting, whose long, spiny vines of jealousy choke the joy out of me. Yes, that happens, and then I do nothing but stand in front of the mirror and give my brain permission to go there. To that place of entanglement. The place where thoughts of comparison sit and wait to be embraced.

The more I compare, the emptier I become.

And the more I compare, the emptier I become. So empty.

And empty women, oh how we come unglued.

Especially when the empty settles in the part of our souls where unmet desires restlessly wait. And in that dark corner, desperation churns for what could be but isn't, and what we want but still don't have.

What do we long for? A romantic, attentive mate. A true and trusted friend. A child. Then a child who makes me look good. An attentive parent. A certain talent. Opportunities, things, feelings, recognition, body size, financial freedom, a beautiful house ... the list lengthens.

We long for "it" and the deep satisfaction surely found in getting "it." And when others around us get "it," we pretend we are happy for them. We make the good girl in us act happy. Maybe part of us is sincere. Maybe not. But in the quiet of the bathroom, the gnawing becomes a splitting plow. Oh, how it digs and cuts and unearths the inside of us.

The "J" Word

I don't struggle with jealousy often. But when it does sneak into my heart, it's a terrible feeling. Do you agree? Research shows there's a perfect storm of conditions that seem to come together when jealousy occurs. According to a Yale University study, social-comparison jealousy occurs when the following three conditions are present: (1) a person receives negative personal feedback (2) in a domain of life that is important to them, and (3) they believe another person is performing successfully in that same domain. In the study, those who experienced social-comparison jealousy were found to disparage the other person and experience feelings of depression and anxiety.[6]

I've had many "its" in my life. And for each, these three conditions were present. I felt the sting of rejection or negative feedback in an area that was important to me and watched as other people seemed to be effortlessly blessed in this very area.

The daddy "it": If only he would have stayed. I felt unwanted.

The boyfriend "it": If only I had a date to the dance. I felt ugly.

The friend "it": If only I could be friends with her. I felt left out.

The life management "it": If only I could get it together. I felt incapable.

The better behaved kids "it": If only I could be a better mom. I felt inadequate.

The opportunity "it": If only a publisher would give me a chance. I felt overlooked.

Unwanted. Ugly. Left out. Incapable. Inadequate. Overlooked. Now there's an attractive set of issues to pack in my little TJ Maxx-clearance-rack leatherette purse and tote around with me.

I let these comparisons and the anxiety they create negatively affect my relationships, my mood, and my confidence to pursue my dreams. The ugly truth is, comparison steals celebration. And a life void of celebration is a life empty. We stop celebrating our own good and have a really hard time celebrating others' good.

Which is just what I did thirteen years ago when me and my little issue-laden leatherette purse headed off to a writers' conference.

I mentally crafted the script of how it would come together for me there. Surely some publisher would see something in my writing worth taking a chance on and this time things would turn out differently. This time I'd leave feeling like I was wanted, beautiful, included, capable, and noticed.

I made plans to meet up with my friend Laura for dinner after the conference and couldn't wait to share a bit of good news. Surely there would be some after all my meetings that day. But the actual script didn't follow my wishes. And by the time I waved Laura over to the table I was saving, I felt rubbed raw by my vulnerability. Laura plopped down in her chair and said hi with such breathless enthusiasm I wanted to gag. And in that moment, I hated that we'd made dinner plans that night. Even more than that, I hated my desire to gag. How awful am I?

I stuffed the gag deep down and scolded that feeling with a quick *shame on you.* I smiled. I braced myself. And I reminded myself that I loved Laura and should be genuinely happy for her. Laura was a talented writer. Gifted at stringing together unexpected words in ways that captivated and moved a reader. I wasn't surprised her publisher appointments at the conference had gone so well.

"Three!" She squealed. "Three publishers asked to take my proposal with them. Can you believe it? They said they had a *really* good feeling about my chances with their pub boards."

Pub board. The place where a writer's dreams sparkle into reality or crash and burn. Oh, the power in a simple yes or no. For a writer, the difference between those two words can have a soul soaring to the moon or sinking to the depths of the deepest deep.

She was soaring. I was sinking. My publisher appointments were quick, curt, and void of any hint of sparkly hope. At all. And so off I went into the restaurant bathroom, staring in the mirror at a woman splitting open, drowning in comparisons, and feeling the weight of empty.

No jealous thought is ever life-giving.

We get empty when we park our minds on comparison thoughts and wallow in them. Nothing good grows in this place; as James 1:15 says, "Then, after desire has conceived, it gives birth to sin; and sin, when it is full-grown, gives birth to death." No jealous thought is ever life-giving. Wallowing in jealous thoughts actually leads to death. Death of contentment. Death of friendships. Death of peace. And certainly death of joy.

Jealousy and envy cut deeper and deeper until we bleed empty. We lose perspective on what we do have and soon focus only on what we don't have. It's at this point that we sit back and say, "Okay, I get all that. I know this is truth. I know jealousy isn't good. It's not as if I enjoy it, ask for it to haunt me, or even want it in my life. But it's there. So, what's a girl to do? Just having someone say *don't feel jealous* doesn't help me. Having someone point out a fault without offering a solution just makes me feel even more unglued."

Amen to that. And the best solution I know — the only solution I know — is pure truth from God's Word.

The Galatians verses about reaping what you sow are part of a larger passage that offers some revealing teaching. It includes a two-step plan of action for when we're struggling with jealousy: we need to carry our own load (Galatians 6:4 – 5), and then carry some love to others (Galatians 6:9 – 10).

Carry Your Own Load

The first step in dealing with jealous thoughts is to focus on our own responsibilities and actions. For in this focus we find reasons to celebrate what we have been given and what we are doing right.

> Each one should test their own actions. Then they can take pride in themselves alone, without comparing themselves to someone else, for each one should carry their own load. (Galatians 6:4 – 5)

In my book *Becoming More Than a Good Bible Study Girl*, I shared a truth I challenge myself with when jealousy comes knocking: "I'm not equipped to handle what she has, both good and bad — and what she has is always a package deal of both." In other words, I've been assigned a load I can handle. The good and bad in my load is what I should carry. I'm not designed or assigned to carry someone else's load.

Consider the Galatians verses again from *The Message*:

> Make a careful exploration of who you are and the work you have been given, and then sink yourself into that. Don't be impressed with yourself. Don't compare yourself with others. Each of you must take responsibility for doing the creative best you can with your own life.

I like the thought of "doing the creative best with [my] own life." When I wish for someone else's life, I waste the limited life energy I've got to face my own challenges and opportunities. God has a beautiful plan for me — a creative best I can accomplish with my life.

Isn't it just like Satan to want to distract me from this? Satan is a liar who steals, kills, and destroys. He wants to steal my attention, kill my joy, and destroy my creative best by making me want what God has entrusted to someone else. In other words, it is a lie straight from Satan that I'd be happier and more content with someone else's load. I wouldn't. It may feel like I would, but feelings are tricky things. Remember that dinner with my friend Laura? Well, she did get a book deal. And things went well for her.

I didn't get a book deal, and it forced me to spend a few more years learning the craft of writing and getting my young family to a place where they could handle the demands of a mommy under the pressure of a book deal. Had I gotten a book deal at the same time as Laura, it would have been disastrous for me on many levels. Mostly, it would have been awful on the writing front.

I recently went back and read some of that early book proposal. I sat right down and thanked God from the deepest places in my heart that those words never went public for all the world to read. I wasn't ready. I see that now. And I thank God for the protection.

There are many areas of my life I can look back on and thank

God for the protection. The boys who never asked me out. The strong-willed tendency in my daughter that eventually turned into a passionate tenacity for missions. The opportunity I never got that keeps me humble. All the things I have and don't have are what make up the unique load I've been assigned.

Ultimately, that's why God tells us to concentrate on carrying our own load and avoid comparing and striving for someone else's load — it's for our protection. I see that now. It gives my brain a better place to go when those I-want-what-she-has thoughts start choking the joy from me. And instead of feeling empty, I feel a sense of possibility. I drop seeds of my own creative design and watch the long limbs of purpose start to form.

Carry Some Love to Others

Although I arrest jealous thoughts by focusing on my own load, I don't stop there. The next step in dealing with comparisons is to actively pursue good for others. We find this teaching in Galatians 6:9–10:

> Let us not become weary in doing good, for at the proper time we will reap a harvest if we do not give up. Therefore, as we have opportunity, let us do good to all people, especially to those who belong to the family of believers.

My friend Sara showed me one of the most beautiful examples of carrying some love to others that I have ever experienced. If anyone could have chosen the route of the empty woman and been jealous of others, it would have been her. But she chose a different path. And though a terminal disease threatened to empty her dry, this young woman stayed filled to overflowing. She carried her own load. She carried love to others as well.

Not too long ago, I sent Sara a text message. It was especially hard to write because I knew the minute I hit "send," it would be the last message I would ever send her. I whispered good-bye. And with that, the words went where I couldn't go. Based on an email that same day from someone close to her, I knew Sara would soon be with Jesus.

"Beautiful Sara ... oh, friend, you will forever be a picture of lavish grace to me. I will never see the word *grace* and not think of you. I so wish I could glimpse how glorious you will look holding Jesus' hand soon. Whole. Healthy. Happy. But so very missed."

Sara wove her love, encouragement, and grace throughout the blog world. That's how I met her. I started seeing lots of comments from "Gitz" pop up on my blog and thought it was a fun nickname. Her comments always made me smile. So, I clicked over to her blog and her story made me cry.

Sara had been sick for a long time. She told her story this way:

> I have lived in this condo since I was 29 years old. I haven't left it, ventured out, even opened a window in years. It's where I am, where I will always be, and yet when someone says the word "home" I don't think here. I don't think anywhere, really. I think who. Because my home rests in the hearts of people.[7]

Though Sara lived in pain and isolation, she took time to write amazing notes of encouragement. To me. To many others in the blog world. That's grace, lavish grace.

Grace ... effortless beauty ... a favor rendered by one who need not do so. She, the one who was in such need, became the one who gave and gave.

One of her emails to me said, "i love how you can drive a really good point home while still making me laugh silly." I knew every letter she typed took effort, so much effort. She never used capital letters but always wrote complete thoughts. Encouraging thoughts. Thoughts I will miss.

Just a few weeks before Sara took a turn for the worse, I went on a writers' retreat with my friends from the *(in)courage* blog. We're just a group of girls who connect through writing blogs on this terrific site hosted by DaySpring. Sara was a vibrant part of this group, but because she wasn't able to leave her condo, she couldn't join us. At least not in person. But we determined she could join us via Skype.

Together, we huddled in a circle around a laptop and took turns looking into the screen and exchanging what we suspected might be treasured last words. Last giggles. Last glimpses. And when I took my turn to love on her, she instead spent time loving on me. She just wouldn't have it any other way.

Tears welled up in my eyes as I reached out to touch the screen. Several of us reached out to touch the screen—to connect with the only bit of Sara we could. Then we turned the computer around so Sara could see the beach. The ocean deep. The sky wide. The sun radiant.

No words were necessary. God's creation said it all. He goes deep like the ocean. He stretches wide like the sky. He reaches out like the sun. Even when our tears slip, we know His hand never does. Since I know that full well, I didn't say "Good-bye, Sara." I simply whispered, "Until then, my friend ... until then."

In the meantime, I'm sitting my soul at Sara's feet so that I can learn from her. This fulfilled woman could have been so empty, so needy, so tempted to look around at the blessings of others and think those entangling comparison thoughts waiting in the shadows of her soul. But Sara refused to sit in that dark corner and wallow in what she didn't have.

Instead, she celebrated what she did have. From that place, she sowed life and reaped a deep and rare soul satisfaction. And from that rare place, a woman who never left her condo spread her goodness around the world.

Sara went to be with Jesus shortly after I finished writing this chapter. She will be forever loved and missed, but never forgotten. The way she chose to live taught lessons that will linger on for many, many years. May it be so with us as well.

A jealous spirit or a giving spirit? The choice is truly ours.

I don't want to be an empty woman — a woman set up to come unglued. And I suspect you don't want to be an empty woman either. How might it change our perspectives if we realized that the life we have and sometimes wish we could exchange for someone else's is a privileged life — one many others would give anything to have?

A jealous spirit or a giving spirit? The choice is truly ours.

How might you carry your own load and carry it well today? How might you carry some love to others and expand your soul's capacity today? Oh, that we make the choice to carry our own loads and carry some love to others. Choose these ways over gnawing, clawing, soul-atrophying ways of wanting the illusive "it." Refuse the pull and drain of the empty woman's ways. Even when life is hard and chaotic, I pray we make the courageous choice to embrace what is and to fill our souls with all of the good reality right in front of us.

What I am. What I *do* have. What I *can* do.

And when I think of *her* and who she is and what she has and what she can do? And it splits me open like a plow cutting a line in the soil to sow seed? May the seeds harvest sincere celebration for her and complete peace in me. Me. A woman once so empty and unglued. Learning. Growing. Reaping more and more fulfillment.

10

Negative Inside Chatter

It's time to tackle negative inside chatter—those misguided thoughts that can easily turn into perceptions that then all too easily turn into dangerous realities. And realities based on runaway feelings rather than truth always lead to one thing—insecurity.

You are not liked.

Who are you to think you could do that?

Why did you say that? Everyone thinks you're annoying.

Your kids just illustrated every inadequacy you have as a mom.

You are invisible.

Have you ever been taunted by thoughts like these? I have. Why do we let such destructive words fall hard on our souls? Toxic thoughts are so dangerous because they leave no room for truth to flourish. And lies are what reign in the absence of truth.

The other day I was discussing something with my husband and I said, "I know you think I'm being annoying and overly protective about this, but ..."

Art stopped me and said, "How do you know that's what I'm thinking? Please don't hold me liable for saying things that are really only thoughts in your mind."

Wow. His challenge stopped me dead in my tracks. Somewhere in our relationship, something had set off negative inside chatter that said, "Lysa, he thinks you're annoying." Because I didn't call that thought into question right away, I gave it free rein to turn into a perception. That perception then became the filter through which I processed future conversations we had. I started conversation-hunting for more and more evidence that would prove he thought I was annoying. As I built layer upon layer of these skewed confirmations, the thought "I'm annoying" became my reality. But it *wasn't* reality. It was a wrong thought turned into a wrong perception that became a false reality.

Art was so right to stop our conversation and untangle my statement. *He* hadn't said those things. I assumed he was thinking them and I operated as if those toxic thoughts were coming from him. Bless his heart.

I think we girls do this way too often. All these toxic thoughts collect and ratchet up the negativity inside. The more ratcheted up this negativity gets, the closer we are to an explosion (spewing) or an implosion (stuffing). Whether we spew or stuff, our anxiety level skyrockets, affecting not only our minds but our souls and bodies as well. Want to know how?

I'm about to quote some research findings that are crucial to add here, especially for those of us who are interested in physiology and how God designed our bodies. It's complicated stuff, so don't get lost in the midst; just hang on for a few lines while I share what some really smart people are saying about some really amazing stuff.

> When we take in information in our body and activate an attitude —a state of mind—it influences our reaction to life. The then-activated attitude—positive or negative—is transmitted from the thalamus (which is like the air traffic controller for all the thoughts in our brain) down to the hypothalamus.[8]

The hypothalamus, an organ roughly the size of an almond, is a mini chemical factory in our brains where our thought-building processes happen. Signaled by the larger (egg-sized) thalamus to prepare a response to our thoughts, the hypothalamus determines the type and quantity of chemicals released into the body, thus greatly impacting how we function emotionally and intellectually.[9]

For instance, if you are anxious or worried about something, the hypothalamus responds to this anxiety with a flurry of stress chemicals. These chemicals engage the pituitary gland — the master gland of the endocrine system. The endocrine system in turn secretes hormones responsible for organizing trillions of cells in your body to deal with impending threats. Negative thoughts shift your endocrine system to focus on protection and limit your ability to think with wisdom or to develop healthy thoughts.

On the other hand, if you change your attitude and determine to apply God's excellent advice not to worry, the hypothalamus prompts the secretion of chemicals that facilitate feelings of peace, and the rest of the brain responds by secreting the correct "formula" of neurotransmitters that facilitate clear thinking.[10]

In short, God designed our bodies to respond to our thoughts. Negative thoughts lead to a crisis response — activating us physically but hindering our thinking. Positive thoughts allow us to process a situation accurately and respond in a healthy way.

This truth challenges me to hold my thoughts to a higher standard. How dare these runaway thoughts be allowed to wreak mental and physical havoc! How dare they simply parade about as if they are true, feeding our anxieties, and manipulating us into feeling insecure, inadequate, and misunderstood! Oh how much trouble we invite into our lives based on misguided assumptions.

Because God made our bodies — and all the emotions, hormones, and chemical responses they contain — His Word provides wisdom on how to manage it all. Here is a key piece of wisdom written by the apostle Paul:

> Do not be anxious about anything, but in every situation, by prayer and petition, with thanksgiving, present your requests to God. And the peace of God, which transcends all understanding, will guard your hearts and your minds in Christ Jesus. Finally, brothers and sisters, whatever is true, whatever is noble, whatever is right, whatever is pure, whatever is lovely, whatever is admirable—if anything is excellent or praiseworthy—think about such things. Whatever you have learned or received or heard from me, or seen in me—put it into practice. And the God of peace will be with you. (Philippians 4:6–9)

You've probably read this passage before. But have you thought of applying it to your thoughts in light of all we've just learned about the science of how our minds work? God knew all along how important it is to guard against anxiety by planting our hearts on thankfulness and inviting His power into our lives. His peace is not just a spiritual blessing, but a physical one as well. Interesting, isn't it?

We are to park our minds on constructive thoughts, not destructive thoughts ... thoughts that breathe life into us, not suck life from us.

We are to think about, ponder, and park our minds on constructive thoughts, not destructive thoughts. Thoughts that build us up, not tear us down. Thoughts that breathe life into us, not suck life from us. Thoughts that lead to peace, not anxiety.

Three Questions

So, here are three questions we can use to hold our runaway thoughts, assumptions, and misperceptions in check. We'd do well to ask them of ourselves when thoughts we assume others are thinking drag us down.

QUESTION 1: Did someone actually say this or am I making assumptions about what they're thinking?

People aren't thinking about us nearly as much as we might think they are. And even if they really are thinking something negative about us, we can deal with it once we know the truth. When we assume something about another person's thoughts, that's unfair to the person and unnecessarily damaging to ourselves. Instead of staying anxious, we need to seek out truth by asking the person for clarification and asking God to help us process what we hear in the right way.

Philippians 4:6 invites us to choose prayer over worry in every situation. Instead of allowing our thoughts to overtake us, whether in assumptions or despair, we can ask God to shine His truth into our situation: *Do not be anxious about anything, but in every situation, by prayer and petition, with thanksgiving, present your requests to God.*

QUESTION 2: Am I actively immersing myself in truth?

The more we read God's truths and let truth fill our minds, the less time we'll spend contemplating untruths. Thinking runaway, worrisome thoughts is just an invitation to anxiety. Thinking on truth wraps our minds in a peace that rises above our circumstances. Remember what science reveals: When we feel anxious, those "negative thoughts shift your body's focus to protection and reduce your ability to process and think with wisdom or grow healthy thoughts."

Thinking runaway, worrisome thoughts is just an invitation to anxiety.

If we want truth to guard our hearts and minds, we have to immerse ourselves in truth. We do that by opening God's Word and letting God's Word open us. That's how we are made new in the attitude of our minds.

Philippians 4:7 holds a promise for us when we turn to God and allow His truth to fill us — our hearts are protected by peace: *And the peace of God, which transcends all understanding, will guard your hearts and your minds in Christ Jesus.*

QUESTION 3: Are there situations or relationships that feed my insecurities?

Finally, if some situations or relationships feed our insecurities, maybe we need to take a break from them for a season.

I was in the grocery store once when I ran into one of those insecurity-feeding friends. She asked if I would be attending the school's fundraiser that weekend. I told her I'd be contributing, but I had a speaking engagement and wouldn't be at the actual event.

Her response shot out like a dagger straight to my heart: "I don't know how you leave your kids like you do. I could never do that."

I quietly pretended as if I needed to rearrange the contents of my cart in order to avoid eye contact while she finished unloading her opinion. I could have said, "I'd love for you to help me understand what you just said," and then given an assured, non-emotional, Jesus-has-settled-this-issue-in-my-heart answer. Instead, I ended the conversation as quickly as possible, cut short my shopping trip, headed to the car, and cried. I questioned whether or not I was a good mom. I doubted my judgment about missing the school fundraiser. I held up my imperfections to the seemingly perfect daily performance of my accuser and felt woefully inadequate in comparison.

I later tried to talk to this friend about what she'd said. But it became painfully obvious that she could not support my decision to do ministry outside the home. And eventually, after getting stung by several other hurtful comments, I discerned that our relationship was as bothersome to her as it had become to me. We had to agree to disagree and eventually the friendship faded away. The friendship was not characterized by honor, encouragement, and love. Therefore, it wasn't good for either of us.

My initial reaction in the store almost started a domino effect of condemnation. Instead I chose to think about what God had already revealed to me as His will for this time in my life. I didn't need *her* approval on my obedience. Only God's. This, per the teaching of Philippians 4:8, is where I parked my mind: *Finally, brothers and sisters, whatever is true, whatever is noble, whatever is right, whatever is pure, whatever is lovely, whatever is admirable—if anything is excellent or praiseworthy—think about such things.*

Quieting the Inside Chatter

If honor, encouragement, and love are the characteristics of the friendships I want in my life, I need to foster these qualities in my relationships. One way to do this relates to the matter of inside chatter.

We engage in inside chatter when we hyper-analyze a conversation after the fact. The back-and-forth in our heads sounds something like this:

When I said this, she probably thought that.

Now she probably thinks this.

Maybe I should say something to fix it, but then she might think I'm a crazy overanalyzer.

Oh good grief, why did I say that?

If you don't know what I'm talking about, then throw your hands in the air and praise God right now that you don't struggle with the demon of inside chatter. But if you do know what I'm talking about, exhale with relief that you're not alone.

Now that you've exhaled, let's inhale a new possibility. The possibility that we can foster the honor, encouragement, and love we desire by giving our friends permission to quiet their inside chatter. What does that look like? It might be just a quick phone call to say, "When you and I have had a conversation, you don't ever have to worry about how I'll analyze everything later. I'm not thinking you're crazy or high-maintenance or wacky, okay? I love you. And if I need clarification about something, I'll just call and process it with you." What a gift a phone call like this would be to a friend who has been driving herself crazy over a conversation the two of you had recently!

Inside chatter is such a crazy thing. Last week, I had a funny conversation with a friend. We were having coffee when she admitted she'd been having inside chatter about something she'd said to me on the phone the night before. She went to bed kicking herself for saying something she felt was dumb and was certain I thought she was a bit wacky.

I absolutely didn't go to bed thinking she was the least bit wacky. Quite the opposite. I went to bed thinking she is one of the cutest, nicest people I know.

Friendships are like plowed open fields ready for growth. What we plant is what will grow. If we plant seeds of reassurance, blessing, and love, we reap a great harvest of security. Of course, if we plant seeds of backbiting, questioning, and doubt, we reap a great harvest of insecurity.

Indeed, today is a great day to call a friend and say, "I love you. That's all I'm thinking. Period."

The more love and joy I pour into others, the more I experience in my own life.

I've discovered that the more love and joy I pour into others, the more I experience in my own life. But I have that overflowing joy — that super-abundant joy — only when I focus on God's truth and His Word. Psalm 126:2–3 would make a lovely lead song for the soundtrack of our lives:

Our mouths were filled with laughter, our tongues with songs of joy. Then it was said among the nations, "The LORD has done great things for them." The LORD has done great things for us, and we are filled with joy.

Not that everything is always peachy. Good gracious! I know this is tough stuff. I know these issues can be more complicated than three simple questions. But holding our thoughts accountable is a good place to start.

Addressing the issue of inside chatter will lead us to freedom. Not just freedom *from* negative things like doubt and insecurities, confusion and suspicion. But freedom *to* pour out love on others. Freedom *to* think clearly. Freedom *to* obey God's call on our lives no matter what others think. Our thoughts really matter.

After all, how a woman thinks is often how she lives.

I think we need to read that one again, don't you? How a woman thinks is often how she lives. May we think on and live out truth, and only truth, today.

My Soul Needs to Exhale

The other day I was in the kitchen with my teenage son. I was going through the mail. He was stirring a pot of rice. It was a rare, quiet moment in our house where all the other kids were gone so I wanted to make the most of an opportunity to talk.

"Mark, what are you thinking about?"

"Nothing," he replied. And I knew from the gentle way the word slowly tumbled out, it wasn't a brush-off. But how in heavens could he be thinking about nothing?

I had to know. "So, when you say nothing, do you really mean nothing? Or do you mean you are thinking about something you don't want to tell me about?"

"No. I mean I'm really not thinking about anything right now."

"How is that possible? Like you don't have one thing you are worried about or a conversation you're rehashing or a bunch of lists you are mentally reviewing in your mind?"

He tilted his head and looked at me like I was one giant, unplucked eyebrow. "Ummm ... nope."

Amazing. Truly amazing. And challenging. I think I need to be a little more like Mark when it comes to emotional white space.

His brain can actually rest.

Wow.

Rest. That sounds so good, but it's really difficult for a girl like me. Even when my physical body is at rest, my mind rarely is. Can you relate?

I feel like I'm always juggling balls in my brain. Kids' needs. Home demands. Work projects. The to-do lists never stop.

Yet the Bible makes it very clear that we are to pursue rest. Literally we are to hit the pause button on life once a week and guard our rest. Guard it fiercely. Guard it intentionally. Guard it even if our schedules beg us not to.

Resting is definitely not something I have mastered. I am not the hero example of this chapter. I'm just a messenger who has been trying to make some imperfect progress in this area. Because I know where there is a lack of rest, there is an abundance of stress. And where there is an abundance of stress, there is great potential for me to come unglued.

Where there is a lack of rest, there is an abundance of stress.

Always being on the go and keeping my stress level ratcheted high is a huge internal trigger for me. I know it. Now, I'm trying to follow God's advice on what to do about it.

Time to Exhale

Sabbath rest has always been part of God's plan for His people:

> "If you keep your feet from breaking the Sabbath and from doing as you please on my holy day, if you call the Sabbath a delight and the LORD's holy day honorable, and if you honor it by not going your own way and not doing as you please or speaking idle words, then you will find your joy in the LORD, and I will cause you to ride in triumph on the heights of the land and

to feast on the inheritance of your father Jacob." For the mouth of the LORD has spoken. (Isaiah 58:13–14)

Yes, Sabbath. I love the way the word sounds. It resonates deep within me, and it's something I know I need.

Sabbath is the time set aside for my soul to breathe. Really breathe. So much of my daily life is inhaling, inhaling, inhaling— taking so much in and holding my breath hoping I can manage it all. But we can't just inhale. We must also exhale—letting it all out before God and establishing a healthier rhythm by which to live.

Even though I'm not very good at it, I love that God wants us to rest. I love that He's not just interested in what we do but also in making sure we don't get burned out. God reminds us to Sabbath so we'll have new rhythm in our everyday. This is one twenty-four-hour period to disrupt our typical rhythm so we'll be set up to *find our joy in the LORD*.

I don't know about you, but when I'm coming unglued, I feel like I've lost my joy. So, anything that will help me find joy, especially soul-resonating "joy in the LORD," sounds so good. My soul exhales with one long "Yes!"

If this is what I want—to find my joy in the Lord—the Bible makes it clear that *rest* is key.

I must physically slow down. Stop. Pause. Yes, I am called to rest. But I am also called to reflect. If we are honoring the Lord's holy day, we're called to rest from three things:

- Going our own way;
- Doing as we please;
- Speaking idle words.

How this looks for you might be different from how it looks for me. But one thing I know is that God is much more concerned with the attitudes of our hearts than the actual activities of our bodies on the day of Sabbath. We must absolutely avoid the crippling effects of legalism by which we pride ourselves in following rules, all the while missing out on actually following the Lord. The apostle Paul reminds us:

> Therefore do not let anyone judge you by what you eat or drink, or with regard to a religious festival, a New Moon celebration or a *Sabbath day*. These are a shadow of the things that were to come; the reality, however, is found in Christ. (Colossians 2:16–17, emphasis added)

I love that the Scriptures remind us that the reality of true Sabbath is found in Christ. In Him we see a picture of grace. And in grace we can be vulnerable enough to be completely honest *with* ourselves *about* ourselves.

Completely honest.

Sabbath will be unique for each person.   There are honest, personal reasons we need to observe the Sabbath that will be unique for each person. There are private reflections and conversations we need to have with God. There is a desperate need for us to hit pause, sit with God, and ask Him to reveal some things to us.

Where am I going my own way right now?

What area of my life is more self-pleasing than God-pleasing?

What idle words need to be reined in from running rampant in my mind or spilling from my lips?

And when I see these questions from Isaiah 58, something profound occurs to me. The Sabbath isn't just a time to be *ob*served; it's a time to be *pre*served.

The observer remembers to rest.

The preserver rests to remember — remember that it's all about God.

It's all about pausing. It's all about connecting with God without the distracting rhythms of our everyday. Letting God show us a better rhythm. One that will preserve the best of us and reveal the places we're getting off track and being filled with unnecessary clutter.

Once we see clutter — the places we're going our own way, the areas we're more self-pleasing than God-pleasing, the idle words that need to be reined in — we can clean the clutter.

The observer remembers to rest. The preserver rests to remember — remember that it's all about God.

The Sabbath does this.

In a sense I take this one day for a soul cleaning so I can live the other six with the freedom to breathe that my soul so desperately needs.

Freedom to breathe. Space to breathe. Inhaling and exhaling in a gentle rhythm set by God. This is what my son Mark is really good at. It's not just that his brain can rest and think no thoughts. He really knows how to embrace space for his soul to breathe.

And you know what? I've never seen Mark come unglued. Never. This is partly because he has a beautiful temperament. But it's also because he knows what it means to find his joy in Christ. In grace. In Sabbath. Once I asked Mark, "How is it you don't get angry when your brother does something to annoy you?" He replied, "Simple. If he's getting on my nerves, I just tell him not to do that. And if he keeps doing it, I walk away." He inhales the issue but exhales with grace.

Alrighty then. No need to get all angry and complicated and overanalyzing. Just an honest assessment from a soul that is rested enough to stay calm. Joy, rest, grace. Yes, I want more of this Sabbath.

My friend Bonnie Gray calls this process "finding your spiritual white space." In the visual arts world white space refers to portions of a page left unmarked. Bonnie says, "In graphic design, white space is a key element to the aesthetic quality of a composition. The more fine art a composition is, the more white space you'll find. The more commercial a piece is, the more text and images you'll find crowded in. The purpose is no longer beauty. It is commercialization."[11]

I don't want my life to be so crowded that I'm nothing more than a commercial for crazy.

I don't want my life to be so crowded that I'm nothing more than a commercial for crazy. That's how I feel sometimes. But that's not what I want. I want to be fine art.

Like the *David* we talked about earlier. Chiseled and perfected with time.

Time with the One who, from the beginning, modeled Sabbath. Time with the One who can see past my façade and into the deep places of my heart. Past the surface reasons I come unglued to the deeper places.

And in that space of time, with the One who really sees and knows, I'll rest and I'll reflect.

Three Sabbath Questions

As I reflect, I dare to ask the three questions prompted by the prophet Isaiah.

QUESTION 1: Where am I going my own way right now?

Sometimes it's hard to see areas in our lives where we are going our own way instead of God's way. Honestly, these aren't the deep thoughts my mind is consumed with while running to Target, filling my car with gas, or rushing to get the kids to school on time. But these are the areas I can and should consider on my Sabbath. That's when I have time to stop the rush and to pray and think — really pray and think. Not just for short-term survival but for the ongoing revival of my soul.

Then when I start going my own way, I'll be able to recognize it and stop it.

God's way is love, joy, peace, patience, kindness, goodness, faithfulness, gentleness, and self-control (Galatians 5:22–23).

My way looks so much different. Just take all those qualities and flip them into a package that's impatient, rushed, and pushed to the limits. It's not pretty and it's not what I want. I want God's way. Heavens knows I do.

But when the rhythm of my soul is survival instead of revival, I will come unglued.

Last year I got into a terrible habit of letting my Sabbath slip. And it came out in horrific displays of raw emotions. Oh, I was pretty good at hiding these displays from everyone else, but I spewed on those I love the most.

Once my daughter needed new athletic shoes, so off we trotted to our local shoe store. It should have been a wonderful bonding time, but instead I quickly found myself becoming snappy. The first thing that caught me off guard was the high price tag of the shoes. Don't these athletic gear companies know we are in a recession?

The second thing that sent my attitude teetering on the edge was the fact that she can't use these shoes for anything but this one sport . . . and they can't be worn outside . . . and she'll need another pair for gym class. Hello mac-and-cheese-for-dinner every-night-this-week so my daughter's feet can be all they can be for middle school sports.

Then my daughter tells me she must try on the shoes with socks. We didn't have socks. The store didn't have any to loan us. Now we had to buy socks, which would add eight dollars more to our already high tab.

Urggghhhh.

Once we bought the socks and got the shoes on her feet, she was frustrated with how they fit. So, she tried another pair. And another. And another. And — oh, for crying out loud — just pick something, would you!

Suddenly I felt very frayed. It was as if every nerve in my body suddenly climbed to the surface of my skin and started demanding we go home right this instant or my head might explode into a thousand particles of pixie dust.

Nothing about me was loving, joyful, peaceful, patient, or gentle. Nothing said, "This woman loves Jesus, serves Jesus, spends time with Jesus." I just went my own way by letting my raw emotions have their way.

Can you relate? Have you ever been in that shoe-store scenario? Here's a great verse to consider:

> Follow God's example, therefore, as dearly loved children and walk in the way of love, just as Christ loved us and gave himself up for us as a fragrant offering and sacrifice to God. (Ephesians 5:1–2)

The Message says it this way:

> Watch what God does, and then you do it, like children who learn proper behavior from their parents. Mostly what God does is love you. Keep company with him and learn a life of love.

Ahhh ... keep company with Him. Sabbath. Learn a life of love ... Sabbath.

This is what the rhythm of Sabbath shows me. I can learn a life of love. Joy. Peace. Patience. Kindness. And all the other qualities of God. When I pause once a week to realign my way to God's way, my soul exhales, and it is good. Sabbath, oh how my soul needs this.

QUESTION 2: What one area of my life is more self-pleasing than God-pleasing?

> May these words of my mouth and this meditation of my heart be pleasing in your sight, LORD, my Rock and my Redeemer. (Psalm 19:14)

We live in a day and time when our rights sometimes take precedence over our pursuit of righteousness, when we get caught in the rush of seeking self rather than seeking God.

So quick to offer a complaint when things don't go exactly right.

So forgetful with our thank-yous when things go well.

And I am challenged by this.

My husband owns a Chick-fil-A restaurant. If there were ever a man who cared to the depth of his being about serving his customers, well, it's my man. To him it's not just about serving a great chicken sandwich. It's about serving a life. It's his opportunity to hand his customer a sandwich with a smile, a kind word, some kind of go-the-second-mile gesture, and for that brief moment, he makes their day a little brighter, a little better.

And he never qualifies his kindness.

The grumpy customer gets the same kindness as the happy one.

He inspires me. He is a God-seeker in his business. A self-seeker would simply see each customer as another transaction. A God-seeker sees each customer as a person with real needs. He always offers the rare word of kindness, encouragement, and blessing.

It's not just my husband who views customers this way — it's a fundamental value in the corporate culture of Chick-fil-A. I've sat in many a meeting with the executives of this company, and God-seeking is modeled through every aspect of the business. Interestingly enough, Chick-fil-A is also one of the few retail businesses left in America that still honors the Sabbath. They are closed on Sunday. A day of rest. A day of reflection. A day to regroup and focus on God and family.

I truly believe Chick-fil-A is blessed with seven days worth of business in the six days they are open.

Might I dare to be a Sabbath woman who is more God-seeking than self-seeking? Might I be a woman of the rare word of kindness?

And might I even be so bold as to not just make kindness come out of my mouth but also be the meditation of my heart?

It's not easy. But it is good.

So here's the challenge I've issued myself: Remind myself on the Sabbath day to find the good in my everyday.

In every situation, in every interaction, in every day, be a noticer of the good. That's what God-seekers do—they notice the good. Even when the good has nothing to do with the circumstances and everything to do with how God will teach us through them—find the good. And in that good, our soul will exhale, "Sabbath."

QUESTION 3: What idle words need to be reined in from running rampant in my mind or spilling from my lips?

The New American Standard Bible translates "idle words" in Isaiah 58:13 as "speaking your own word." We get into trouble when, instead of parking our minds on *truth*, we let them idle in *perception*. Boy, is this dangerous!

I believe this danger is yet another thing God wants to protect us from in the Sabbath—the day to be preserved.

When I first got married, I was desperate to be a "good wife" and determined to figure out how to do it well. So, I took note in my head of what a "good wife" does:

- She cooks meatloaf.
- She vacuums every day so there are lines in the carpet indicating its cleanliness.
- She sticks love notes in his briefcase.
- She buys and wears lingerie.
- She likes wearing lingerie and wears it a couple of times a week.
- She gives him his space when he gets home.
- She hangs up the phone when he walks in the door.

- She learns facts about football and watches games with him.

- She prays for him every day.

And the list grew and grew.

Eventually, the list in my head of what a good wife does so completely overwhelmed me that I cried. I felt inadequate. I started to shut down. I constantly felt unglued.

I assumed the list in my head was in my husband's head too.

I grew bitter. And in a moment of complete exhaustion, I yelled, "Your expectations are ridiculous!"

To which he replied, "What expectations?"

"The list ... the list of hundreds of things I need to do to be a good wife," I sobbed through the snot and the tears.

His blank stare dumbfounded me. He had no such list.

It was a perception. These were idle thoughts allowed to run rampant in my mind for so long I confused them with truth. The truth in 1 Corinthians 13 reminds me love is patient, kind, not proud, and keeps no record of wrongs. I had so broadened my scope of things to do that I had diminished my vision of simply loving my husband.

Do less. Be more. Clear out the clutter of idle words. Find that white space. Honor God.

If I would have been practicing regular Sabbaths, at which times I sought God on this issue, I suspect I could have saved myself years of coming unglued in my marriage. Years.

Finally, I went to my husband. "Honey," I said, feeling the entanglements of expectations loosening their grip on me, "I can't do everything good wives seem to do. But I can do three things. So, tell me your top three things, and I will do those well."

After all, I could spend a whole marriage doing a hundred things halfway with a bitter attitude and an overwhelmed spirit. Or, I could do three things wholeheartedly with a smile on my face and love in my heart.

His three things were simple: Be an emotionally and spiritu-ally invested mom with our kids, take good care of your body and soul, and keep the house tidy. (Notice he said "tidy" — not perfectly clean.) That's it.

He could care less about home-cooked meals. He is fine with me hiring someone else to vacuum the carpet. And he's totally okay if I watch 48 Hours while he watches man-cub events on a different TV.

Now, he didn't say anything about lingerie. But, he could argue that it is a subplot of my taking good care of my body. The problem is, I'm much more of a sweatpants kind of girl. Yes, Victoria has a little secret, and I haven't a clue what it is.

But that's a topic for another day entirely.

For today, I've narrowed my scope to three things, and this nar-rowing has broadened my vision for a great marriage.

I am a three-things wife. It's simple. But simple is good. And, more importantly, I stopped sabotaging my marriage by stopping the idle thoughts.

How might this help you? How might this improve some of your relationships?

Letting Your Soul Breathe

I know that any Sabbath changes — whether it's realigning our way with God's way, being a God-seeker looking for the good, or stop-ping the idle thoughts — won't happen overnight. But the more we intentionally practice Sabbath, the more the Sabbath rhythm will become natural to us. Inhale. Exhale. For this is the rhythm of the soul that breathes and lives; it is the rhythm of the soul that doesn't just survive but thrives!

So, can I encourage you to seriously consider implementing some version of what we've discussed? And might you go ahead and pen-

and-ink schedule your Sabbath time to rest and reflect this week, whether on Sunday or another day?

As I said before, the Sabbath isn't just a time to be observed, it's a time to be preserved. The observer remembers to rest. The preserver rests to remember. Remember, it's all about God. Capture this Sabbath time. And then do it again next week. And the next. Yes, this unglued woman is determined to make Sabbath one of the most crucial parts of my imperfect progress.

> *The more we intentionally practice Sabbath, the more the Sabbath rhythm will become natural to us.*

It Isn't All Bad

I know coming unglued—spewing or stuffing raw emotions—isn't good. It causes hurt and damages relationships. The hurt is real, deep, and lingering. I don't negate that in any way. But I also want to acknowledge that coming unglued isn't all bad. And I pray that after reading this chapter you'll say the same thing.

Now let's pretend you and I are sitting at my sticky farm table talking about all this stuff face-to-face. I'd have in front of me a file folder of items I've collected that I want to show you. A blog post from a friend named Jenni. A note from a friend named Sharon. And a couple of emails exchanged by Samantha and Abby. You'd notice that these pieces of paper have little grease spots and probably a jelly stain or two that I'd try to smear away with licked fingers. And in the midst of all that, we'd chat. First, let's chat about taking an honest look at some places inside our souls we might not have peeked at recently.

An Honest Peek Inside the Soul

I've lived in the same house for twenty years. That's my whole married life. My husband and I have wonderful plans for things that

need to be repaired, updated, or remodeled. We work as a team …
to call in the professionals. That's right. We have gifts and talents but
carpentry, wiring, and plumbing are not among them. Those things
get hired out.

My friend Jenni and her husband are different. They know how
to do amazing house repairs and remodeling projects that completely baffle me, including fixing plumbing leaks, sealing grout,
replacing bad wiring, and repairing dry wall.

One of Jenni's recent blog posts captivated me. Thoroughly
impressed by the work they'd been doing on their house, I was completely inspired by the correlation she drew between that work and
the necessity of looking at our deep underneath. "Our underbelly,"
as Jenni calls it. Here's what she wrote:

> I get embarrassed some days when friends come to check on our
> progress, and I'm afraid it doesn't look like much.
>
> I long to rush to the decorating and make every room invit-
> ing for friends. But I would be covering up bruises, bumps,
> and blemishes that will eventually show through. Doing all the
> tough work on the underbelly will pay off down the road when I
> know all the pretty decor is not covering up anything but rather
> enhancing the architecture.
>
> And this is exactly what the underbelly of my life looks like.
>
> Isn't this what we do in our personal development and spiri-
> tual lives? We are in such a hurry to look good that we put on the
> pretty "decor" to appear as if we're all together, but so often we
> don't take care of the underbelly. And, man, this is hard work.
> Some days it doesn't seem like I've gotten very much done …
>
> I still get offended when someone asks a question in a way
> that makes me feel like I've failed. I still want to retaliate when
> someone hurts me. I still get insecure when I don't feel comfort-
> able. I still get jealous when someone else accomplishes the thing
> I dream of doing.

> The underbelly takes tough work that isn't always immedi-
> ately visible but it's the foundation to our health — emotionally
> and spiritually.[12]

Yes, Jenni, it is. But we'll never see what needs to be repaired
and cleaned up in our underbellies unless we do what Jenni and her
husband did with their fixer-upper house. They looked.

We don't do that very often with our underbellies, the deep
insides of ourselves. We're just trying to survive without losing it
again. Maybe it's because we're busy or maybe it's because we don't
know how to look. Well, I think I've discovered at least one place we
can start looking — our unglued places.

Might our unglued places be like windowpanes of clear glass
that give us an honest peek inside our souls — places where we can
see what's really going on within? It's the same principle Jenni and
her husband apply to remodeling their house. They know they have
to deal with underbelly things, such as bad wiring, before hanging
pictures and arranging furniture. They have to fix the foundational
issues first.

We need to do the same. In the last chapter, we read about pausing
once a week to let our souls exhale during a Sabbath rest. That's good
and necessary. But what about the other six days of the week? How
are we supposed to stay calm and exhale in the midst of the everyday
messes when we so desperately want to be "together" women?

In my pursuit to present the image of a "together" woman, I
might do many things — volunteer on lots of committees, outfit my
girls with matching dresses and bows, show up on time, pluck my
eyebrows and shave my legs, drive a clean car, and hang a seasonal
wreath on my front door. Then I could pat myself on the back and
think, *Ahhh ... I am together. I've decorated my life with impressive
stuff.* But behind closed doors, the decorations will be meaningless
in the face of my emotional outbursts or the silent treatment I give
my husband.

A well-decorated life isn't a sign of togetherness. It may seem impressive temporarily, but in the long run if the foundation crumbles, it won't matter how many pretty pictures are on the walls. The whole house will fall.

This is why coming unglued isn't all bad. Just as a light that fails to come on when the switch is flipped may indicate a wiring problem, coming unglued may indicate a problem with our internal wiring. Outward expressions are internal indications. If our outward expressions are unglued, there's some brokenness internally. Broken places we won't address unless we are forced to acknowledge their existence. As painful as it might be to name these broken places, seeing ourselves — really seeing, deeply and honestly — is a very good thing.

Outward expressions are internal indications.

When I look through the window of my unglued reactions, I may find pride I don't want to acknowledge. Longstanding unforgiveness. Deep-seated bitterness. Simmering anger. Joy-stealing jealousy. Condemning shame. Haunting regrets. Entangling rejection. Or I might see a schedule crammed too full and have to own up to feeling taken for granted and unappreciated. Or it could be that I finally acknowledge the very real damage never-ending stresses have caused — that I sometimes both love and despise my life at the same time. And I can't stand that I feel this way. Why do I feel this way?

If things are ever going to get better, we have to acknowledge our underbellies that fuel our unglued reactions. We may not like what we see, but at least we'll know what we're dealing with. We can call it what it is and ask God to help us.

I'm tired, God. What do I do?
I'm lonely, God. What do I do?
I'm mad, God. What do I do?
I'm insecure, God. What do I do?
I'm frustrated, God. What do I do?

I don't take time to ask God what to do often enough. Do you find this to be true? Perhaps having a clear-eyed view of our underbellies will help us go to God more — more frequently, more authentically, more humbly.

Coming unglued isn't all bad if it brings us to God.

Therefore, might we agree that coming unglued isn't all bad if it brings us to God? And brings to light what's eating away at us in the dark? But even more, might we agree that coming unglued is glorious if the end result of that brokenness leads us to holiness?

Looking at My Own Underbelly

Have you ever been in a situation in which something small feels really big? Maybe a look from someone that suddenly makes you feel they don't like you at all. Perhaps a friend doesn't return your phone call, and you feel like it's an indication that you're not important. Or your child makes a comment about how terrific another mother is and you feel like it's a direct indication of their disappointment in you.

Usually these things aren't true. The look was just a look with no hidden meaning. The missed phone call was just a slip on your friend's to-do list. The comment … well, maybe that one was a dig. Or maybe it was just a compliment for the other mom and not a statement against you. If we're not careful, these misguided feelings can distract us, discourage us, and trigger past pain to start taunting us.

It happened to me the day after Thanksgiving last year. My sister Angee and I got up at 3 a.m. and were in line at a certain retail establishment thirty minutes later. I know. I agree. That's crazy. But like a hunter stalking prey, I was after something. You see, I'd been having this little issue with my washing machine — or maybe I should say my *unwashing* machine. My teens put their dirty clothes in, and the washer gave them back wet but still dirty. That's slightly problematic when your people like to wash their clothes after *every* wearing.

It's not so problematic for me. I'm the queen of rewearing stuff. You might be shocked if I told you how many times I rewear my jeans before washing them. It's a little nuts. But it doesn't bother me a bit. My kids, however, are not like me. They are a little over the top about their definition of clean. My sister has this same overactive cleaning situation going on. My mom calls it her "AC/DC." (Um, no, Mom, that's a rock band. It's called OCD.) Anyhow.

At the 3:30 a.m. hour, there we stood in line. I was after the buy-one-get-one-free washer and dryer. Angee was after a half-priced computer. When the store doors opened at 5 a.m., we both scored. Happiness abounded. Then we left to get some breakfast before continuing our shopping. This is the part of the story where the happiness faded.

In the drive-thru, my credit card was "not approved."

Let me get this straight. It *was* approved at the store just five minutes ago when I made a major purchase. But now for a little two-dollar bundle of egg, cheese, Canadian bacon, and English muffin, suddenly I'm *not* approved?

Not approved.

Not *approved*.

Ouch.

My sister wasn't fazed a bit. She whipped out cash, paid for my breakfast, and we headed to the next store on our list. But those words, "not approved," hung like a black cloud over my head. It bothered the stink out of me. I knew it was just some sort of technical glitch, but that's not what it felt like.

When that girl leaned out of the drive-thru window and in a hushed tone said, "I'm sorry, ma'am, but your card keeps coming up as not approved," it felt personal. Really personal.

Suddenly, my past pain and current embarrassment started running its mouth inside my head. *You're nothing but a loser. You are unwanted. You are unloved. You are so disorganized. You are poor. You are not acceptable. You are not approved.*

Do you see how those small things can suddenly feel so big? Do you see the subtle shift happening? It went from my credit card not being approved to *me* not being approved. There it is. The unglued feeling coming on strong. Remember we talked about how all that negative inside chatter is a huge red flag that things internally are about to set me up for a raw reaction externally!

I didn't explode at the drive-thru girl or the credit card company, but I stuffed this horrible feeling down inside of me. Like the insidious beginnings of soul leprosy, it started eating away.

I felt it.

And combined with how tired I was by that afternoon, my emotions were heightened to the danger zone. All it took was a little comment from one of my kids about how much better their Aunt Angee did blah-blah-blah and wham! I lost it.

I yelled. I threatened. I pursed my lips and pointed my finger.

And then I hated myself.

Right there in the midst of a family where I'm supposed to be a "Christian example," I blew it. Why, why, why had I blown it? Dadgum, what is my problem? In my head, I again heard the hushed admonishment of the drive-thru lady, "Not approved."

I wish I could tie up this story in a nice bow and give you a pretty ending, but I can't. It was anything but pretty. I felt awful. And I went to bed wondering if the Lord Himself might come down and say, "Lysa TerKeurst, I have had enough of your immature reactions. You are no longer approved to be a Bible study teacher. Look at you!"

> *Our Lord doesn't whisper hushed condemnations. Convictions, yes. Condemnations, no.*

But that's not the Lord's voice. Our Lord doesn't whisper hushed condemnations. Convictions, yes. Condemnations, no.

I crawled into bed and stared wide-eyed into the darkness that enveloped the room. "Give me Your voice, Jesus. I need to hear You above all this mess. If I don't hear You, I'm afraid this darkness is going to swallow me alive." Nothing came. I couldn't hear a thing. So I had a choice. I could lay there in the dark replaying the awful events of the day, or I could turn on the light and read God's Word.

When lies are swarming and attacking me like a bunch of blood-thirsty mosquitoes, the best thing I can do is open God's Word and immerse myself in His truth. Lies flee in the presence of truth.

Did you catch that? Lies flee in the presence of truth. But just as we have to flip on a light switch to erase the darkness, we have to activate truth to erase the lies. We have to capture our thoughts, hold them up to the truth, and make them line up with Scripture before we entertain those thoughts. Here's how I do this:

THOUGHT: *I am a horrible mom.*

VERSE: "We take captive every thought to make it obedient to Christ" (2 Corinthians 10:5).

TRUTH: *I am not a horrible mom. I might have had a horrible reaction, but that doesn't define me.*

THOUGHT: *I didn't react like a good mother would. And I certainly didn't react like a Christian.*

VERSE: "Whatever is true ... think about such things" (Philippians 4:8).

TRUTH: *I love my kids. That is true. I love God. That is true. I was tired. That is true. I felt insecure and it affected me. That is true. God gives never-ending grace. That is true. I can ask for forgiveness and redeem this mess. That is true. The more I think on truth, the quieter the lies get. That is true.*

THOUGHT: *This will never get better. I'll always be a slave to my raw emotions.*

VERSE: "Set your hearts on things above . . . set your minds on things above" (Colossians 3:1–2).

TRUTH: *I'm tired of setting my heart on the voice of the enemy. Setting my heart and mind on lies is like setting the radio dial on a trashy station — what feeds me affects me. So, here is my heart, Lord. I set it on truth and truth alone. Here is my mind, Lord. I set it on truth and truth alone.*

I read these same Scriptures over and over and over. And I let them feed better thoughts. I've learned that anytime I start hearing lies speaking louder than truth, it's an indication my soul is starving for God's Word. So I fed it truth and I starved it of the lies begging to get down deep and mess me up.

The next day I made a quick call to the credit card company and assured them there was no fraudulent use of my card — I was the one buying a washer and dryer at 5 a.m. the day before. After the credit card company was assured of the truth, they once again approved the use of my credit card. But even better, after being assured of God's truth, I felt approved again.

I then saw an opportunity to model Christ's teaching even in the aftermath of my awful reaction. I asked for forgiveness from my family. And though I'd totally blown it the day before, I realized God's grace always allows for second chances. Instead of wallowing in the pit of what had been, I stepped out into imperfect progress and holiness.

A Step toward Holiness

That was one step in the direction of holiness. Holiness. Is this even possible for a girl like me? I saw that it was. So, I say it is. And so does

God. "Therefore, if anyone cleanses himself from what is dishonorable, he will be a vessel for honorable use, set apart as holy, useful to the master of the house, ready for every good work" (2 Timothy 2:21 ESV). Cleansing myself from what is dishonorable. Yes, that is what I want. But I can't cleanse what I don't see.

Oh, that I will see my raw emotions as a call to action. Some imperfect progress needs to be made right here, right now. Yes, if coming unglued enables me to see my underbelly, then there is a good and redemptive side to it. And if it all ultimately points me to what Isaiah calls "the Way of Holiness" so that I spend less and less time unglued, then it's not merely good, it's of God:

> And a highway will be there; it will be called the Way of Holiness; it will be for those who walk on that Way. The unclean will not journey on it; wicked fools will not go about on it. No lion will be there, nor any ravenous beast; they will not be found there. But only the redeemed will walk there, and those the LORD has rescued will return. They will enter Zion with singing; everlasting joy will crown their heads. Gladness and joy will overtake them, and sorrow and sighing will flee away. (Isaiah 35:8–10)

I hope I might one day silence the howling sorrow of regret. And stop the sighing of a soul so spent. A soul that catches herself thinking she will never get better. Is it possible? Might all this imperfect progress and awkward steps toward holiness — these hidden treasures of unglued — be leading me to a place where I experience gladness and joy more than sorrow and regret?

My friend Sharon Sloan just emailed me this morning telling me of her experience of discovering a hidden treasure in an unglued moment.

> Last night as I sat on my kitchen floor sobbing, surrounded by a pool of tears and encircled by backpacks, textbooks, and

lunch boxes, I was unglued. Outwardly unglued, yet inwardly broken. Broken before Him. Beautifully broken. I had spent the day "Driving Miss Daisy," or in this case "Miss Eileen," my sweet mom who had just surrendered driving privileges. I was spent, exhausted, and broken. Then I had to deal with the kids — football, exams, homework — and hubby . . . sweet hubby.

In the ugliness of my unglued self, I realized the blessing of being unglued. . . . If we let it, unglued will allow us to become humbly and beautifully broken before Him. I pray I am more often broken and less often unglued. But if unglued leads me to being broken, I am thankful.[13]

Oh yes, yes, yes, my friend! This is it. This is the upside to our downfall. Indeed, coming unglued isn't all bad. It lets me see two crucial things. It lets me see me — really see me. It also lets me see others — really see others.

And when others come unglued on me, I must remember their external expressions are internal indications as well. Brokenness is there. And while I may not feel tender and gentle toward their unglued expressions or reactions, I can be tender and gentle toward their brokenness.

They Have Underbellies Too

This stinks. That's usually my first thought when someone starts to come unglued on me. Maybe they send an ugly email or text. Maybe they make a little passive-aggressive statement that doesn't feel very little. Maybe they stop calling and make it obvious they're avoiding me. Maybe they say hurtful things about me behind my back. Whatever their sign of unglued, it feels bad.

Basically, they are being critical of me. Sometimes criticism is fair. Maybe I messed up, and it would serve me well to reconsider. Other times, criticism is nothing but rotten spew. And boy does it stink. But if I get stuck in the stink, it serves no good purpose.

Might there be another way to look at harsh criticism? To get past the hurt so I can see if they have underbellies I should consider?

The other day I Googled the word *underbelly* and stumbled upon an article about the armadillo lizard. This fascinating creature has scales that are hard and pointy and have "Don't mess with me" written all over them. But, like all tough creatures, this lizard has a vulnerable place.

The armadillo lizard's tough exterior wraps around its back but softens at the underbelly. When threatened, the lizard grabs its tail and displays a prickly, intimidating posture to keep other creatures away. At that point, the rest of its body serves only one purpose — to hide and protect its most vulnerable part.

So, what does this strange desert creature have to do with criticism?

In an effort to protect my underbelly, I sometimes get all wrapped up in myself and tragically forget the underbelly of my critic — the place they are vulnerable and what they might be hiding and protecting beneath their harsh words and prickly exterior. This is a place they may never let me see. It's a storage place for their hurts and disappointments. It holds the root cause of their skepticism and the anger that probably has very little to do with me. Remember, "For the mouth speaks what the heart is full of" (Matthew 12:34b). And from the overflow of their underbelly, they spewed.

If I forget the other person's underbelly, I am tempted to start storing up my own hurt, skepticism, anger, and disappointments. If I remember this underbelly, I have a much greater chance to keep it all in perspective.

What if the criticism isn't just a meaningless, hurtful experience? What if God is allowing this to use me for good if I'll let Him? Oh, I know this isn't easy. I'd much rather God send me on a mission trip to help build a house than walk through this process of examining my issues — and of being willing to be used by God to help a critical, hurting person.

It's hard. But, it's godly. We are called to represent Christ wherever we go, to all those with whom we interact. Therefore, we re-present Him with each encounter. If I handle myself well, I'm reminded in Luke 21 that this will result in me being a witness for Jesus to this person: "And so you will bear testimony to me [Jesus]. But make up your mind not to worry beforehand how you will defend yourselves. For I will give you words and wisdom that none of your adversaries will be able to resist or contradict" (vv. 13 – 15).

Did you catch that part about making up our minds beforehand? Before we're in the midst of the hard situation, we need to make up our minds. That's what we're doing in this chapter as we consider our underbellies and their underbellies. We're deciding in advance not to worry. Not to get all defensive. And to gather God's words and wisdom.

How easy it is to type those words and how hard it is to live them out!

But let me share a story that might provide a picture of what it means to do this in everyday life.

I recently received an email from a woman named Abby who was deeply offended that my ministry didn't do more to encourage women in her specific situation. As a working mom, she struggled with the stresses and strains of trying to contribute to the support of her family while still taking care of her children. She had been listening to our radio program for a while and felt disappointed in our lack of encouragement for working moms. Here's what she wrote:

Dear Proverbs 31,

Are you aware that you surely have many working mothers as listeners? I was raised in a very conservative family, so this arrangement is odd to me and not at all easy. However, it really seems to be where God has us right now. Unfortunately, your ministry is one of the worst regarding having encouraging words for a working mother in my situation.

What was so ironic about the criticism in this email is that I'm one of those working moms. Granted, I work from home much of the time, but I surely know the stresses and strains of running a home and running a ministry. Even when I was reading this email I was simultaneously packing lunches on a kitchen counter splattered with juice, crumbs, and jelly blobs. Two of my kids were complaining that we never have any good snacks and fussing about who would get the last juice box. Another was trying to convince me it was perfectly safe for her to ride in a car with her girlfriend who'd just gotten her license.

In the midst of all this, I felt as if a neon sign were flashing in front of me broadcasting the message: "Your ministry is one of the worst ... worst ... worst!" That word *worst* wove its way into my heart like a snake in the grass. "Worst!" "Worst mom." "Worst lunch packer." "Worst ministry." "You are the worst!"

Wait a minute ... I've been around this mountain before and I'm not going there again. Yes, what were those truths I used in that credit card situation?

"We take captive every thought to make it obedient to Christ" (2 Corinthians 10:5).

"Whatever is true ... think on such things" (Philippians 4:8).

"Set your hearts on things above ... set your minds on things above" (Colossians 3:1–2).

I stopped the "worst" thoughts by realizing that this was a hard statement made by a woman in a hard situation. It said a lot more about Abby's hurt than it did about me or my ministry. Yes, I remembered the underbelly. And I recognized I had other pressing things like juice boxes and kid attitudes to deal with in that moment. So I called Samantha, one of my ministry staff members, and asked her to pray about a gentle response to Abby. I knew Samantha wouldn't spew back hurt from hurt. She'd see the evidence of hurt in Abby and respond tenderly to that hurt.

Samantha wrote this beautiful email response:

Dear Abby,

We appreciate you bringing your concerns to us. It's always good to hear our listeners' thoughts about the content of our shows. We take each suggestion we receive into consideration.

I wasn't able to determine which show you heard. If you could let me know which specific shows didn't set right with you, that'd be most helpful.

It sounds like you're a hard worker and have much on your plate with your full-time job, husband, children, and home. We understand the complexities and unique circumstances that come with being a full-time working woman. Actually, we're in your shoes as well! We each wear many other hats for our families, friends, churches, and Proverbs 31 Ministries as well.

Sweet sister, know that we not only have walked the road you're on, we're on it right next to you! Our shows and ministry as a whole are based on bringing God's peace, perspective, and purpose to every busy woman. We aim to keep them applicable to women in different stages and areas of life.

May I pray with you?

Lord, thank You for Abby and her desire to honor You with her finances. Thank You for giving her the heart and compassion to care for her family and her work. It sounds like she's gifted and oh so capable. We ask that You give her moments of sweet rest in between all her hard work. And please provide a way for her and her family to pay any debt off quickly. Bless Abby with more of Your truth and peace and joy. In Jesus' name, Amen.

Thanks again, Abby, for touching base and for your suggestions on topics for our radio spot.

May the Lord bless you with His peace today.

Samantha

A few hours later, Samantha received a response from Abby. It offered a rare glimpse into the underbelly of one woman's hurt. My heart melted. And our suspicions were right — her original email wasn't really about us. These kinds of emails rarely are. It was about other things festering deep within. Here is what Abby wrote:

Dear Samantha,

I was very touched by your thoughtful response. I apologize for what I now realize is perhaps projecting messages I've heard over the years from other sources onto Proverbs 31 Ministries.

Your response made me realize that, despite my prayers for help in this area, I still have some bitterness/anger/resentment that I need to deal with in a proper manner.

Thank you also very much for your prayer. It means a lot to me. I will pray for your ministry as well. Perhaps someday, God willing, I can reach out to others in a more meaningful way as well.

Precious sister, this isn't easy stuff, but it is good. It's a crucial part of our imperfect progress. With each of these types of encounters, we are given an opportunity to put on display that Jesus is the Lord of our hearts and the Lord of our reactions. Therefore we must remember that Jesus teaches, "Bless those who persecute you; bless and do not curse" (Romans 12:14).

Do you care to join me in seeing this unglued progress as good? To affirm how it can be good for us, good for our responses — and possibly even good for others who see Jesus in us?

To do this, we must dare to pray for authentic hearts. Not that we welcome the critical person into our inner circle and start doing daily life together. But it is a rare and beautiful thing when we choose to offer love in situations when most people would choose to scorn or ignore.

Dare to pray for an overwhelming sense of God's love — not love for the ugliness that has come from this person but love for the soul God created within them. She or he belongs to God. He loves them. He treasures them even when He doesn't approve of their actions. He treasures us even when He doesn't approve of our actions. Thanks be to God!

And I wonder ... in the midst of giving what we might consider an undeserved gift of love, could our eyes be opened to a different perspective? Might we see something we desperately need to see — about

> *It is a rare and beautiful thing when we choose to offer love in situations when most people would choose to scorn or ignore.*

them, about ourselves, about our Jesus? Might we make the choice to be ruled more by Jesus' commands than by our feelings in that moment? "But I tell you, love your enemies and pray for those who persecute you" (Matthew 5:44).

When someone says something ugly about me, I try to consider the source. That's great advice that we've all heard, right? But wouldn't it be wonderful if a person receiving an undeserved gift of love from me also considered the source? And saw not me, but the Jesus who reigns inside of me? It would be just like what the Bible reveals in Acts 4:13: "When they [the rulers and elders of the people] saw the courage of Peter and John and realized they were unschooled, ordinary men, they were astonished and they took note that *these men had been with Jesus*" (emphasis added).

Oh, let it be so noted about my life! That my words, my love for those who love me — and even more, my love for those who don't love me — reveal that, yes, I have been with Jesus.

Me. The unglued woman who dared to look at her underbelly and saw some hard-to-see things:

Wounds.

Broken places.

Possibility.

Change.

Steps toward holiness.

Imperfect progress.

The hurt in those who hurt me — their underbellies.

Grace.

Love.

Me looking a lot more like Jesus than I did before.

And to discover through all this seeing — being unglued isn't all bad.

Accepting the Invitation
to Imperfect Progress

L ast week I literally had to stand at my kitchen counter and decide if I was going to extend grace and laugh or come completely unglued. It was a choice plain and simple. And honestly, that's what all this comes down to, doesn't it? A choice.

Can you relate?

Of course you can. That's why I love you so.

It was about the graduation invitations that went forth from our home. They were late, and they were ... different than what I expected. My son didn't bring home the form to order the proper pieces to complete the invitations. So, instead of printed name cards, there was a scribbled name. Instead of a cap-and-gown photo, there was a resurrected eighth-grade photo that had been cropped so the 2005 at the bottom didn't make the recipients do mental math while scratching their heads.

And I certainly know that you are supposed to have two envelopes —an outer and an inner. However, if you mess up the outer envelope and have no extras, you might be forced to use the inner envelope with no sticky strip by which to seal it. So, please excuse the marks left behind from the purple glue stick used for this emergency.

As I stood at the counter, I bossed my heart around a little and in the end decided to let a truth from Proverbs 3 redirect me a bit.

> Never let loyalty and kindness leave you! Tie them around your neck as a reminder. Write them deep within your heart. Then you will find favor with both God and people, and you will earn a good reputation. (vv. 3–4 NLT)

I didn't want loyalty and kindness to leave me. I'm not exactly sure about binding them around my neck, but I'm all about writing them deep within my heart. So I memorized this verse ... or at least I got the gist of it in my mind and on my heart. And it helped.

While our invitations look a little squirrelly, might you see the love sealed into each envelope? Might you see a mama's heart who is so stinkin' proud of this boy that she decided it didn't really matter what the invitations looked like? Might you hear the laughter sealed into each one because a mama decided the joy of this occasion far outweighs the need for properly done invites?

Besides, my need for proper has certainly been tempered ... and my raw emotions have as well. How about you? Have you been making imperfect progress? Do you still sometimes feel you're more imperfect than progress-making? Me too. But other times I surprise myself and don't come unglued when I know I surely would have before.

I suspect you understand. And that's why I've loved walking through this book with you. It's more than glued-together pages with a spiffy cover. A cover, I might add, that I love. Even though some people have told me they thought the woman on the front was "puking in her purse."

Heavens, I don't like the word *puke*. It's not exactly a cuss word, but I just don't like it. No, the lady isn't sick, y'all. She's coming unglued and screaming into that adorable handbag. And no, that isn't me. People have asked that too. And it makes me laugh.

Anyhow.

Spending these pages with you has created a healing and revealing space for grace in my life. I hope it's been that for you too. A place where we come just as we are without feeling the need to get all gussied up beforehand.

We've certainly lived through some crazy situations in this book, haven't we? The sea monkeys gone bad, the shame-on-you email, a Diet Coke debacle, a woman screaming "bomb" on a plane, and now messed-up graduation invitations.

I bet you've had a few situations in your world as well. Situations that make you ask, "What's the deal, Jesus? Why do I seem to have little pieces of brokenness in my life every day? It's so frustrating. I need Your perspective on this brokenness ... or I need a break from it."

I've prayed those prayers too. Just yesterday as a matter of fact.

A New Charge

With a tired heart, I once again came to the sticky farm table and opened up my tattered and worn Truth Book. My Bible. And what I found gave me the perfect charge for my day. Maybe the perfect charge with which to whisper good-bye to you ... for now. Hear God's Word:

> Sow righteousness for yourselves, reap the fruit of unfailing love, and break up your unplowed ground; for it is time to seek the LORD, until he comes and showers his righteousness on you.
> (Hosea 10:12)

Sow righteousness for yourselves. In other words, sow into your life the seeds of righteousness—right choices that honor God. Make these choices. Choose to honor Him in the midst of it all. Even when you are disheveled, discouraged, or dishonored, honor Him still.

Reap the fruit of unfailing love. Every choice that honors God bears the fruit of God's unfailing love. Remember, nothing can separate us from the love of God (Romans 8:38 – 39). Yet that is Satan's great tactic: to get you entangled in little things that make you forget God's unfailing love. Or, worse yet, doubt God's unfailing love. Resist the distracting entanglement by honoring God with this choice you are faced with right now.

Break up your unplowed ground. Don't resist the blessing of brokenness that tills the ground of your heart. Breaking up the unplowed ground of your heart will make it ready for new life, new growth, new maturity in you.

For it is time to seek the LORD. Seek God like never before. Part of seeking Him is allowing for grace space in your life. Grant God's grace some space in your mind, your heart, your world. How? When circumstances of life leak you dry, see this emptiness as an opportunity. Instead of reacting out of emptiness, choose to see this emptiness as the perfect spot for grace to grow.

> *When circumstances of life leak you dry, choose to see this emptiness as the perfect spot for grace to grow.*

Until he comes and showers his righteousness on you. As you give grace to those who don't deserve it, the mercy jars of heaven will lavish it back on you.

We grow. We are able to make more right choices that honor Him. We start to look at life and people — and annoying circumstances — differently. And we even dare to whisper "thank you" when the need for grace spaces come again and again.

And they will come. The same sweet boy with the messed-up graduation invitations tested the loyalty and kindness I'd just written on my heart — and gave me an opportunity to expand the grace spaces even more when he melted my microwave.

Expanding Grace

Remember the tale of the melted-microwave boy? Well, I think I should tell you the whole story. Have you ever winced at the smell of popcorn cooked too long in the microwave? Worst smell ever, right?

Wrong.

A biscuit wrapped in foil cooked to the point where the inside of the microwave literally melts away — now that's a smell I can't quite describe. It's awful. And I'm quite sure it's toxic on some level. Especially to a mama who can smell if a child dares bring home mint gum hidden in the depths of their book bag. Yes, I have issues with mint. I use cinnamon everything, but that's a story for another day.

The melted-microwave-chargrilled-biscuit smell was the result of a man-child deciding biscuits should cook for a good long while in the microwave. When I scurried to the kitchen to see what in heavens was causing the smell that wafted into my office, my son just shrugged and said, "Huh, I guess the microwave didn't like my biscuit too much."

Two thoughts battled for what should come out of my mouth next.

THOUGHT NUMBER ONE: *I think this situation requires that I pitch a justifiable hissy fit complete with irrational statements like, "How many times have I told you not to put tinfoil in the microwave? You are banned from using the microwave forever and ever and ever and ever. Not even in heaven. I'm telling Jesus not to let you use His microwaves either."*

I'm very mature like that.

THOUGHT NUMBER TWO: *Remember the space for the grace lesson you just learned this morning. You didn't read that Hosea verse just to check off an obligatory quiet time with God. You read it so God could prepare you for what He saw coming. Now let God's truth work in you.*

Make a right choice that honors God.

Don't let Satan separate you from God's best.

Let the tilling of your heart produce a new maturity, a fresh perspective of patience, and whispers of truth in action.

Where this situation is leaking you dry, fill that space with grace. Extend the grace God has so freely given you over and over. And when you do, He'll open up mercy's storehouse and lavish you with even more. His grace never runs out. His grace is completely sufficient.

I felt like acting on thought number one. But I made the conscious choice to let thought number two rein me in. Instead of compounding the problem, I used it as a life lesson. My son learned what a pain it is to rid a house of horrific smells. I suspect he won't be repeating this mistake anytime soon.

But he wasn't the only one who learned something from the burnt biscuit. I learned something as well. I have the capacity to expand the space for grace in my heart. I can be the patient woman I sometimes doubt it's possible for me to be. I just have to choose patience. Or gentleness. Or grace. It's a choice.

I have to choose patience. Or gentleness. Or grace. It's a choice.

Ahhh ... imperfect progress ... soul integrity ... and more space for grace.

I Was Wrong

It was with grace we began this journey, and it is with grace we shall end.

But I must admit, when it comes to God's grace, I was wrong. Wrong about something crucial for us Jesus girls to know and to live.

For years I have struggled with this nagging fear that one day I was going to push things a little too far with God. I would use up all my do-overs and His grace would suddenly dry up. Like the crusty residue on the bottom of a glass, what was once sweet and flowing would now be gone. I would tip the glass of His grace and find nothing but stale air.

I was convinced this would happen because of the secret me who lives in the shadows of my presentable self. The outside me is relatively good, kind, and fairly generous. Not perfect, but she typically remains calm, fun, carefree, and loves to sing out loud. Never mind the real words of the song. Who needs to sing "Feliz Navidad" when "Police nabbed my Dad" rhymes just fine? Ahem.

The outside, presentable me fits with Christian ideals and the Bible verses I memorize. I read the books. I implement the advice. And for the most part, I'm a good friend, wife, sister, and mom. Again, I'm not perfect. But I'm not too bad.

And just when I think the secret me is a distant memory, she steps out from the shadows. She yells. She feels crazy. Or she stuffs and stews. She is a spinning tornado, out of control. She is destructive and chaotic and full of bitter rot. It's an awful feeling to know this tornado looms on the edge of the gentle, easy-breezy girl I want to be.

Out of breath and completely winded, desperate to have the parched places soothed, I'd run to the glass of grace. Time and again, I feared this would be *that* time—the time grace would run dry. The time God would have had enough. The time He would say, "Go away."

I thought God would eventually say that because sometimes a dad says that. Or a friend, a spouse, or someone else we've dared to love. And they mean it. Then they leave or they force us away. They don't leave because of the outside me. They leave because they've caught wind of the secret me and didn't like it. Who can blame them? I don't like her either. And it makes me wonder how God could like her, much less love her.

That kind of thinking is a problem. There aren't two me's. There is only one me. If I start believing that God doesn't accept a part of me, I will in essence believe the lie that God's love is conditional and based on my performance. I will make the outside me try and try and try to perform well enough to earn His love and deserve His grace. All the while trying and trying and trying to quiet the secret me and make her go away.

This split is the core struggle of the unglued woman. The woman in two parts—one good, one bad. One assured, one ashamed. And though she spends much of her time as the good and presentable one, it takes only a little of the secret one to ruin the whole.

But that's where I was wrong. God's grace isn't in limited supply.

The world's economy has limited supplies, but not God's economy.

The world's economy has limited supplies, but not God's economy.

Yes, I was wrong. So very wrong.

And it was Eve, the first woman in the Bible, who helped me to see the truth. Right from the beginning of time, God has dealt tenderly with His girls. Eve was the perfect picture of the unglued woman. Good but bad. Gentle like a breeze, but lured into the tornado of sin.

Do you remember when Adam and Eve ate the forbidden fruit and were banished from the Garden of Eden? Whenever I've read that story, I thought they had to leave paradise because God was punishing them. God was disappointed in them. God was giving them what they deserved.

But I was wrong.

There were two special trees in the Garden of Eden. One was the tree of the knowledge of good and evil. This was the one with the forbidden fruit. The other was the tree of life. This was the one that gave Adam and Eve perpetual life—no diseases, no death, no sagging body parts. (Okay I'm not sure about that last benefit, but I'm banking on this reality in heaven.)

Anyhow.

When they ate of the tree of the knowledge of good and evil, sin entered in the world and it corrupted everything. And at that point, it was God's absolute love and most tender mercy—not his anger or retaliation—that ushered Adam and Eve out of the garden.

They had to leave. If they'd been allowed to stay, they would have kept eating from the tree of life and lived forever, wallowing in sin and all the brokenness sin brings with it. And God couldn't stand that for the people He loved. So, it was His love that made them leave.

And it was God's love and grace that eventually sent Jesus to invite mankind back. Back from our sin. Back from our brokenness. If only we'll proclaim Jesus Christ as our risen Lord, God's grace will never run out.

Brokenness to redemption, where mercy and grace kiss both sides of our face.

Brokenness where we are split open.

Redemption where God knits us back together.

Mercy when we don't get the punishment we do deserve.

Grace when we get the lavish love gifts we don't deserve.

So here we are.

And with my hands I cup your face and say, *God loves you. God loves you now. God loves you when you're unglued. God loves you when you stuff. God loves you when you explode. He loves you when you exemplify soul integrity, and He loves you when you don't. He loves you. He loves you. He loves you. He loves you so much that He refuses to leave you stuck in this place. Take His hand, trust His love, and walk in the beautiful opportunity for imperfect progress.*

Yes, the great unglued will still call for us to entertain its wild and unpredictable realities. But you have been made new, and so have I. So, if by chance you see me in the aisle at Target forgetting this truth and coming a little unglued, just whisper the gentle, hope-filled reminder, "It's a choice. Choose imperfect progress, sweet friend," and smile.

NOTE: Struggles with raw emotions may occasionally reach serious levels. If you or a loved one think you might be displaying unhealthy, even harmful, expressions of anger or depression, please seek out a professional counselor.

Determine
Your Reaction Type

In Chapters 4 – 6 we discussed the four different reaction types:

- Exploder that Blames Others
- Exploder that Shames Herself
- Stuffer that Builds Barriers
- Stuffer that Collects Retaliation Rocks

To help you determine your reaction type, you can take the more extensive assessment at *www.Ungluedbook.com*. But first, complete the simple inventory (pages 194 – 197) to get an initial idea of your reaction type.

When you complete this inventory, concentrate on one relationship at a time. As we discussed in the chapters, our reactions change with different relationships.

1. Think of one person in your life: your mother, spouse, child, boss, etc.

2. When you have a conflict with this person, are you more likely to want to process your frustration outwardly? Or are you more likely to stew about it internally?

   • If you process by stewing or by needing to get by yourself to think before deciding to address it or not, you are more than likely an internal processer with this person and fall into the top half of the diagram below.

   • If you process by talking or yelling about it, you are more than likely an external processer with this person and fall into the bottom half of the diagram.

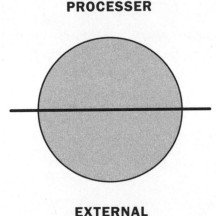

INTERNAL PROCESSER

EXTERNAL PROCESSER

3. Next, think about the way you handle addressing an issue with this person. Are you more likely to talk or argue with them about the issue at hand or to just pretend you are fine?

   • If you are more likely to address the issue, you are an external expresser and fall into the left side of the diagram below.

   • If you are more likely to not address the issue and instead just pretend you are fine, you are an internal suppressor and fall into the right side of the diagram.

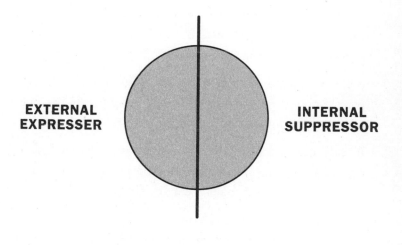

EXTERNAL EXPRESSER   **INTERNAL SUPPRESSOR**

4. Now that you've identified each of these determinants, you can see which quadrant you fall into in the diagram on the facing page and thus identify your reactor type with this particular relationship.

5. Now remember these important things:

- With different relationships, you will likely fall into different quadrants. So thinking about each of your important relationships, retake this assessment for each of them.

- We aren't using any of these labels as condemnations. They are simply gentle convictions that help us see the areas we need to work on. By implementing the strategies in this book, we can be well on our way to having healthier reactions — which means healthier relationships!

- If you are an expresser, there is a really good side to this — your honesty! (See the diagram.) Just remember to balance your honesty with the godly principle of peacemaking.

- If you are a suppressor, there is a really good side to this — your peacemaking ability. (See the diagram.) Just remember to balance your peacemaking with godly honesty.

- The goal of this exercise is "soul integrity," as indicated in the bull's-eye on the diagram. Soul integrity happens when we exhibit honesty that is also peaceable in each of our relationships.

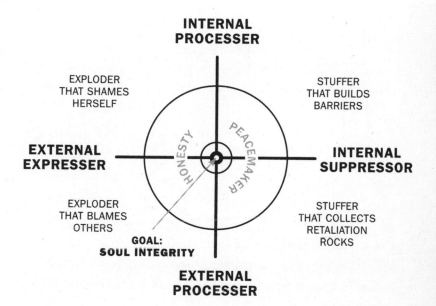

Notes

1. Mike Tiller, "Within These Walls," *My Daily Bread*. Available at: http://www.TheBible.net/modules.php?name=Read&cat=24&ite mid=362.

2. Joshua 5:12–6:20, in *The Bible Knowledge Commentary, Old Testament*, John F. Walvoord and Roy B. Zuck, eds. (Wheaton, Ill.: Victor Books, 1985).

3. Mrs. Charles E. Cowman, *Streams in the Desert*, rev. ed. (Grand Rapids: Zondervan, 1999), September 1 entry; found at http://tinyurl .com/3faply8.

4. Dr. John Townsend, *Beyond Boundaries* (Grand Rapids: Zondervan, 2011), 39–40.

5. Craig Groeschel, *Soul Detox* (Grand Rapids: Zondervan, 2011), 171.

6. Peter Salovey and Judith Rodin (Yale University), "Some Antecedents and Consequences of Social-Comparison Jealousy," *Journal of Personality and Social Psychology*, vol. 47 (1984), 780–792.

7. http://gitzengirl.blogspot.com/

8. Dr. Caroline Leaf, *Who Switched Off My Brain?*, rev. ed. (Nashville: Thomas Nelson, 2009), 52.

9. E. R. Kandel, J. H. Schwartz, and T. M. Jessell, eds., *Principles of Neural Science*, 4th ed. (New York: McGraw Hill, 2000).

10. Leaf, *Who Switched Off My Brain?*, rev. ed., 53.

11. Bonnie Gray, from her forthcoming book *Spiritual White Space* (Revell, 2013) and her blog: "White Space and Soul Rest," http://www.faithbarista.com/2011/03/i-stress-therefore-i-am-10-ways-to-de-stress-soul-rest-series-kick-off/.

12. Jenni Catron, from her blog "Leading in Shades of Grey." The post this was taken from is titled "The Underbelly" found at: http://www.jennicatron.tv/the-underbelly/.

13. Sharon Sloan blogs daily at two wonderful sites: www.histablefortwo.blogspot.com and www.joyinthetruth.blogspot.com

About Lysa TerKeurst

Lysa TerKeurst is a wife to Art and mom to five priority blessings named Jackson, Mark, Hope, Ashley, and Brooke. The author of more than a dozen books, including the *New York Times*-bestselling *Made to Crave*, she has been featured on *Focus on the Family*, *Good Morning America*, the *Oprah Winfrey Show*, and in *O Magazine*. Her greatest passion is inspiring women to say yes to God and take part in the awesome adventure He has designed every soul to live. While she is the cofounder of Proverbs 31 Ministries, to those who know her best she is simply a carpooling mom who loves her family, loves Jesus passionately, and struggles like the rest of us with laundry, junk drawers, and cellulite.

WEBSITE: If you enjoyed this book by Lysa, you'll love all the additional resources found at *www.Ungluedbook.com*, *www.LysaTerKeurst.com*, and *www.Proverbs31.org*.

BLOG: Dialog with Lysa through her daily blog, see pictures of her family, and follow her speaking schedule. She'd love to meet you at an event in your area! *www.LysaTerKeurst.com*.

Also by Lysa TerKeurst

AM I TRYING TO PROVE THAT I'M RIGHT, OR IMPROVE THE RELATIONSHIP?

MY FEELINGS ARE INDICATORS, NOT DICTATORS.

THE ONE WHO HOLDS THE TONGUE, HOLDS THE POWER.

IF THIS IS THE WORST THING THAT HAPPENS TO ME TODAY, IT'S STILL A PRETTY GOOD DAY.

A GIFT JUST FOR YOU

Get these free colorful key tags to keep you inspired and on track. Place your order by emailing: resources@Proverbs31.org and reference "Unglued Key Tags" in the subject line. The only charge is $1 to cover shipping and handling. Bulk orders for Bible studies and small groups are also available with special shipping rates.

ABOUT PROVERBS 31 MINISTRIES

If you were inspired by *Unglued* and desire to deepen your own personal relationship with Jesus Christ, I encourage you to connect with Proverbs 31 Ministries. Proverbs 31 Ministries exists to be a trusted friend who will take you by the hand and walk by your side, leading you one step closer to the heart of God, through:

> • *ENCOURAGEMENT FOR TODAY,*
> FREE ONLINE DAILY DEVOTIONS

> • THE *P31 WOMAN* MONTHLY MAGAZINE

> • DAILY RADIO PROGRAMS

For more information about Proverbs 31 Ministries, visit:
www.Proverbs31.org

To inquire about having Lysa speak at your event, email:
info@lysaterkeurst.com

Made to Crave

Satisfying Your Deepest Desire with God, Not Food

Lysa TerKeurst
President of Proverbs 31 Ministries

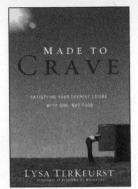

Made to Crave is the missing link between a woman's desire to be healthy and the spiritual empowerment necessary to make that happen. The reality is we were made to crave.

Craving isn't a bad thing.

But we must realize God created us to crave more of Him. Many of us have misplaced that craving by overindulging in physical pleasures instead of lasting spiritual satisfaction. If you are struggling with unhealthy eating habits, you can break the "I'll start again Monday" cycle, and start feeling good about yourself today. Learn to stop beating yourself up over the numbers on the scale. Discover that your weight loss struggle isn't a curse but rather a blessing in the making, and replace justifications that lead to diet failure with empowering go-to scripts that lead to victory. You can reach your healthy weight goal —and grow closer to God in the process.

This is not a how-to book. This is not the latest and greatest dieting plan. This book is the necessary companion for you to use alongside whatever healthy lifestyle plan you choose. This is a book and Bible study to help you find the want-to in making healthy lifestyle choices.

Available in stores and online!

Made to Crave DVD Curriculum

Satisfying Your Deepest Desire with God, Not Food

Lysa TerKeurst
President of Proverbs 31 Ministries

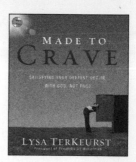

According to author Lysa TerKeurst, craving isn't a bad thing, but we must realize God created us to crave so we'd ultimately desire more of Him in our lives. Many of us have misplaced that craving, overindulging in physical pleasures instead of lasting spiritual satisfaction.

For a woman struggling with unhealthy eating habits, *Made to Crave* will equip her to:

- Break the "I'll start again Monday cycle" and start feeling good about herself today
- Stop beating herself up over the numbers on the scale and make peace with the body she's been given
- Discover how weight loss struggles aren't a curse but, rather, a blessing in the making
- Replace justifications that lead to diet failure with empowering go-to scripts that lead to victory
- Eat healthy without feeling deprived
- Reach a healthy weight goal while growing closer to God in the process

Made to Crave session titles include:

Session 1: From Deprivation to Empowerment

Session 2: From Desperation to Determination

Session 3: From Guilt to Peace

Session 4: From Triggers to Truth

Session 5: From Permissible to Beneficial

Session 6: From Consumed to Courageous

Bonus Session: Moving the Mountain

The *Made to Crave* DVD is designed for use with the *Made to Crave Participant's Guide.*

Becoming More Than a Good Bible Study Girl

Lysa TerKeurst
President of Proverbs 31 Ministries

Is Something Missing in Your Life?

Lysa TerKeurst knows what it's like to consider God just another thing on her to-do list. For years she went through the motions of a Christian life: Go to church. Pray. Be nice.

Longing for a deeper connection between what she knew in her head and her everyday reality, she wanted to personally experience God's presence.

Drawing from her own remarkable story of step-by-step faith, Lysa invites you to uncover the spiritually exciting life we all yearn for. With her trademark wit and spiritual wisdom, Lysa will help you:

- Learn how to make a Bible passage come alive in your own devotion time.
- Replace doubt, regret, and envy with truth, confidence, and praise.
- Stop the unhealthy cycles of striving and truly learn to love who you are and what you've been given.
- Discover how to have inner peace and security in any situation.
- Sense God responding to your prayers.

The adventure God has in store for your life just might blow you away.

Available in stores and online!

Becoming More Than a Good Bible Study Girl DVD Curriculum

Living the Faith after Bible Class Is Over

Lysa TerKeurst
President of Proverbs 31 Ministries

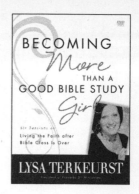

"I really want to know God, personally and intimately."

Those words of speaker, award-winning author, and popular blogger Lysa TerKeurst mirror the feelings of countless women. They're tired of just going through the motions of being a Christian: Go to church. Pray. Be nice. That spiritual to-do list just doesn't cut it. But what does? How can ordinary, busy moms, wives, and workers step out of the drudgery of religious duty to experience a living, moment-by-moment, deeply intimate relationship with God?

In six small group DVD sessions designed for use with the *Becoming More Than a Good Bible Study Girl Participant's Guide*, Lysa shows women how they can transform their walk with God from lackluster theory to vibrant reality. The *Becoming More Than a Good Bible Study Girl* DVD curriculum guides participants on an incredible, tremendously rewarding journey on which they will discover how to:

- Build personal, two-way conversations with God.
- Study the Bible and experience life-change for themselves.
- Cultivate greater authenticity and depth in their relationships.
- Make disappointments work for them, not against them.
- Find incredible joy as they live out their faith in everyday circumstances.

Available in stores and online!

Share Your Thoughts

With the Author: Your comments will be forwarded to the author when you send them to *zauthor@zondervan.com*.

With Zondervan: Submit your review of this book by writing to *zreview@zondervan.com*.

Free Online Resources at
www.zondervan.com

Zondervan AuthorTracker: Be notified whenever your favorite authors publish new books, go on tour, or post an update about what's happening in their lives at www.zondervan.com/authortracker.

Daily Bible Verses and Devotions: Enrich your life with daily Bible verses or devotions that help you start every morning focused on God. Visit www.zondervan.com/newsletters.

Free Email Publications: Sign up for newsletters on Christian living, academic resources, church ministry, fiction, children's resources, and more. Visit www.zondervan.com/newsletters.

Zondervan Bible Search: Find and compare Bible passages in a variety of translations at www.zondervanbiblesearch.com.

Other Benefits: Register to receive online benefits like coupons and special offers, or to participate in research.

ZONDERVAN.com/
AUTHORTRACKER
follow your favorite authors